Bear Encounter Survival Guide

by

JAMES (GARY) SHELTON

Author: James Gary Shelton

ISBN 0-9698099-0-5

Pallister Publishing
Publisher contact: Julie Scheven
Horizon Productions
Box 355
Hagensborg, B.C.
Canada V0T 1H0
Tel/Fax 250-982-2936

Canadian Distributor: Sandhill Book Marketing
#99 - Ellis St., Kelowna, B.C. Canada V1Y 1Z4
Tel: 250-763-1406 Fax: 250-763-4051

U.S. Distributor: Partners Publishers Group
2325 Jarco Dr., Holt, Michigan USA 48842
Tel: 1-800-336-3137 Fax: 517-694-0617

Printings: Nov. 94, Feb. 95, Jan. 96, Jan. 97, Aug. 98, Aug. 99, June 01

Printed in Canada.

Cover photos: Front paw of large male grizzly killed in author's backyard.

BOOK REVIEW
by
Angela Hall, Editor
Coast Mountain News
Bella Coola, B.C., Canada

Over the past years I have published many bear stories in the Coast Mountain News; in our heavily-populated bear area these stories draw a lot of reader interest. Most of the stories indicate the complete helplessness of the individual involved - all of a sudden it isn't the scenario so often portrayed by the common belief "leave them alone, and they won't bother you" or "make lots of noise and they'll go away." Instead, the encounter often becomes a real life-and-death situation where your next decision could be your last.

Unfortunately, until now, there hasn't been much available information about actual bear behaviour. Mr. Shelton's book is timely. He not only addresses the problem, but takes the mystery out of bear aggressive behaviour and gives sound advice on what to do in different situations.

The author's no-nonsense style of writing is not only refreshing, it is based on a lifetime of experience with bears. In this book he includes many bear encounter and attack stories to demonstrate the difficulty of surviving a bear encounter that goes wrong.

During the last 20 years Mr. Shelton has worked on many bear conservation projects, both through our local Rod and Gun Club, and as chairman of the Central Coast Grizzly Management Committee. Currently he has a seat on the steering committee of the South Tweedsmuir Park Atnarko Grizzly Study, and he is also a member of the Bella Coola Valley

Local Resource Planning Committee (L.R.U.P.).

Mr. Shelton has submitted a varying-rotation-age plan to the L.R.U.P. Committee for our Valley that identifies timber plantations, critical wildlife habitat, human settlement areas, and includes consideration for many other values. This plan provides adequate environmental protection without destroying our economic base, and has strategies for reducing human/bear conflict.

He has also spent the last six years developing a bear hazard safety training program which is probably the best in North America. Much of his training material contradicts the endless nonsense about nature that has pervaded our culture in the last 30 years.

This material is long overdue. It is not written by someone within the biological academic community; rather, it is written, as it should be, by someone on the outside - someone willing to fight the tide of unrealistic political trends - someone who puts human life above animal life.

This book provides a fascinating and definitive look at bear behaviour, presents sound advice, and also demonstrates what's wrong with our present beliefs about nature.

If you work or play in the great outdoors, or intend to visit a park in the near future, or just have an interest in bear behaviour, this book is a must.

Angela Hall

Acknowledgments

I would like to thank the following people for helping me wrestle a difficult subject into submission: Julie Pogany, Tracey Gillespie, Angela Hall, Dave Flegel, Harvey Thommasen, Carolyn Foltz, and John Thomas.

No person stands alone in the knowledge he has gained on a subject. I would like to thank Darryl Hodson, Randy Svisdahl, Daryll Hebert, Tom Smith, Tony Hamilton, Stefan Himmer, Peter Clarkson, Helen Thayer, and Jim Hart for sharing their knowledge about bears with me.

I would like to give a special thanks to the Ray family for letting me use the story about their son's unfortunate death.

Please excuse any errors or omissions you find; they are solely my fault.

Contents

Dedication

This book is dedicated to my son, Tyler. Over the years Tyler and I enjoyed many hours together in the bush, hunting, fishing, trapping, exploring, and of course, watching bears.

The last time we hunted spring bear together, in 1990, we had some good chuckles the first day watching two first-year black bear cubs in a determined half-hour wrestling match.

Tyler loved to explore the mysteries of nature, but the modern life of the 1990s was not to his liking. He should have been born to a previous age, an age when young men could still roam free.

Tyler was a realist; he would have enjoyed the contents of this book.

Tyler James Shelton
April 21, 1967 - April 2, 1994

BEAR ENCOUNTER SURVIVAL GUIDE

"To those unfamiliar with the behaviour of bears and indoctrinated by an urban-dominated culture, the creatures are warm, fuzzy, friendly animals. Nothing could be farther from the truth, says Bella Coola bear expert Gary Shelton. In his new book *Bear Encounter Survival Guide*, Mr. Shelton exposes the myths about the unruly ursine and illustrates his points with graphic accounts of bear attacks."

- Robin Brunet, B.C. Report Magazine

Preface

The primary purpose of this book is to provide you with a realistic view of bear aggressive behavior and to outline the most practical strategies for reducing the risk of injury or death during a bear encounter. The secondary purpose of this book is to explain the underlying causes of human/bear conflict and why that conflict is increasing.

In order to accomplish these goals I must take you on a journey through unfamiliar territory, to a place where life-and-death reality reigns and theoretical fantasy is left far behind - a place where the looking-glass of cultural belief is discarded, where the basic elements of nature and animal behaviour are rendered down to identifiable parts.

My views were not derived from being just an observer of nature, but mainly as a participant in nature - a participant who has encountered and studied bears under a variety of circumstances for almost 30 years. My knowledge was earned through direct and sometimes dangerous experiences.

The core of this book breaks new ground and a good portion of my material will be controversial, going against the grain of present trends. There will be some people unhappy with what I present here, especially preservationist biologists.

In the first part of our trek we will explore the complexities of bear behaviour and nature in a way never done before. You will learn a significant body of information about bear aggressive behaviour and how to survive it. You will also gain an appreciation for bears and an understanding of what behavioural traits they must employ in order to survive in a dangerous world - dangers both wild and manmade.

The second part of our passage will be a guided tour through bear management and the wilderness of environmental debate that is presently raging across Western North America. While in this landscape we will see the tactics and misinformation used by desperate people who do not have a clue about what really goes on in nature. You will learn the distinct difference between conservationism and preservationism.

I must deal with all issues that influence human/bear conflict and bear conservation or my critics will claim that the main tenants of my thesis are questionable, because I didn't address all factors related to the subject. If you and I reach our destination together, and in agreement, then I will have convinced you of the following basic points that form the outline of this book:

1. The frequency of different types of bear attacks has been changing, and each type requires different encounter strategies.
2. Bear aggressive behaviour can be categorized, defined, and understood.
3. Predacious black bear attacks are now the most frequent and dangerous type of bear attacks in many areas of North America.
4. Bear avoidance procedures can reduce the frequency of bear encounters, but only to a degree.
5. There are many bear encounters and attacks taking place that biologists and government regulators do not know about.
6. In many of the present encounters and attacks, "playing dead with a grizzly and fighting back with a black bear" *will not work.*
7. Most bear attacks outside of parks, and

some bear attacks inside of parks, are not caused by the victim doing something wrong as many people claim.

8. Contrary to existing misleading information, the populations of bears (both species) are presently increasing in most areas of British Columbia.

9. Rural British Columbians cannot live safely with maximum-phase bear populations.

10. It is possible to adequately protect both humans and bears, and to ensure long-term survival of bear species, by using normal conservation techniques.

There is another very important reason why I must deal with issues related to the way in which we manage bears: If the present trends to preserve bears and to restrict the hunting of bears continue, there will be an increase in danger to people who live and work in the outlying areas of B.C. and in other areas of North America. People will be injured and killed because of the unnecessary radical over-protection of bears.

1

Introduction

In May of 1991 I started three studies:

1. Types and availability of published government pamphlets containing bear encounter and bear attack information.
2. Frequency of predacious black bear encounters in British Columbia.
3. Use of chemical spray deterrents against bears.

Through these I wanted to improve the information in my *Bear Hazard Safety Training Program* for government employees.

After gathering and analyzing all of the bear safety pamphlets I could find, I came to realize how inadequate the available information was regarding bear encounter strategies. Most pamphlets did not even have material from Stephen Herrero's important book, *Bear Attacks* (1985). Those that did contain Herrero's work were either unclear or confusing. After concluding my review in the fall of 1993, I decided that publishing this book was my most important priority for 1994.

In the last 15 years, I have had many dealings with bear biologists in relation to bear research they were working on, or bear conservation projects that I was involved in. The driving purpose behind most bear studies - the preservation of bears - is important and commendable, but with the exception of Herrero's book and a few other biologists' work, the matter of preserving people during bear encounters has been terribly neglected.

Herrero's book raises an important point: Most grizzly bear attacks which result in serious injury or death are defensive-aggresive in nature (the bear feels threatened). Most black bear attacks which result in serious injury or death are predatory in nature, thus the following strategy: "Play dead with grizzly bears, and fight back with black bears." The principle behind this strategy is that when a bear is attacking in a defensive-aggressive manner, it usually retreats when the threat is immobilized or stops moving, but when a bear attacks predaciously, it presses the attack until it kills the victim for food. This basic strategy is important and has saved many lives in recent years, but Herrero never intended this strategy to become the end-all for bear encounters.

I believe there are stronger and better bear encounter survival strategies which are based on my knowledge of bear aggressive behaviour, and also on the following three important facts that I have learned during the last five years of developing my bear safety program:

1. The frequency of different attack categories for both black and grizzly bears has been changing since the mid-1960s.
2. Many bear encounters and bear attacks do not clearly fall into a category where Herrero's basic strategy will work.
3. Those types of encounters and attacks where playing dead with grizzlies and fighting back with black bears *does not work*, have been increasing over the last few years.

I will clarify these points. Prior to 1965 bear attacks in North America were uncommon and basically not understood. Between 1965 and 1978, there was an increase in bear attacks, and those that resulted in serious injury or death were mainly caused by grizzlies attacking defensive-aggressively or predatorily in parks. Between 1978 and 1985 there was a further increase in bear attacks, but the main category which increased was predatory black bear attacks, usually in rural or remote areas. Since 1985 bear attacks have again increased (mainly by black bears), but many attacks by both species were difficult to categorize.

If you carefully analyze the 11 major bear attacks reported in Western North America in 1992, you will discover that in most of these, playing dead with a grizzly and fighting back with a black bear would not have worked.

There are some types of incidents involving grizzly families where playing dead is the wrong thing to do (I'll explain later), and in some predatory black bear attacks the bear is so aggressive that fighting back unarmed or by yourself will not work. Sometimes the people involved cannot tell what species of bear they are dealing with, or the behaviour is such that the encounter type can not be determined.

Most biologists classify bear attacks by the circumstances of the encounter and by looking *back* on the attack with all relevant information considered. I categorize attacks in relation to the type of bear aggression involved, and by looking *forward* on them, using only the encounter information prior to contact by the bear. I also consider the intensity of aggression, usually influenced by how close the perceived threat is to the bear. In other words, biologists are mainly interested in the general category of an attack. I'm primarily interested in whether or not the person involved could have identified the behaviour of the bear and what type of defense strategy would have countered that particular type and level of aggression. I do not attach blame to either the person or the bear when analyzing an attack, and I consider events leading up to the incident as separate but relevant.

My most important departure from the way in which biologists analyze bear aggression is the importance I place on the many bear encounters I have heard about from people where the bear *did not* make contact - what biologists call "non-injurious encounters". This data base is hundreds of times larger than the attack data - and more revealing about bear aggressive behaviour.

In recent years we have seen a tremendous amount of information presented to British Columbians about bears being endangered. This has been an important concern, and in general bears are endangered in most parts of the world. But the truth is that we are now protecting bears to a much greater degree in most areas of B.C. than ever before, and in many areas they have outright protection. This lack of human-inflicted mortality is slowly creating populations of bears that no longer fear man.

There are literally thousands of people who live in bear country who know that if a bold bear is killed, it doesn't come back. They know that wounded bears, surviving family members of bears who are shot, and bears who are dosed with shotgun pellets become fearful of people. It always amazes me when I meet people who cannot accept that this kind of behavioural modification exists.

It is now unacceptable to shoot bears with shotgun pellets, but until the late 1970s this was the most common and effective way of modifying bear behaviour. Some people used pellets because they didn't want to kill the bear, but they wanted it out of their yard, and they wanted it to stay out. I do not advocate the use of shotgun pellets on bears, but it is important for people to understand that this very successful system for changing a particular bear's behaviour is no longer available to us.

We have become used to bears who are afraid of people and who, in many areas, are primarily nocturnal - they have significantly modified behaviour. Most grizzly studies are conducted on this type of bear, so the available data fuels the major misconception that grizzly bears are normally shy, nocturnal creatures. In the last 29 years I have seen the grizzly population in the upper Bella Coola Valley reach maximum level twice. During these periods, many grizzlies became day-active and bold - quite different from what we usually see.

The last time this max-phase grizzly population

Hide of large male grizzly killed in author's backyard Sept. 1983.   *Gary Shelton*

occurred was in the early 1980s. By 1983, family groups of grizzlies were walking down my driveway in the middle of the day. These bears were not garbage-habituated; they were here for the natural attractants including salmon. The situation became so dangerous that local residents lost their normal tolerance and 15 grizzlies were eliminated between September 1983 and August 1984.

I am working hard to create a realistic balance between protecting people and protecting bears, but I have come to realize that human/bear conflict cannot be rendered sensible with only biological studies to go by. Most human/bear conflict data come from park studies, which bias our concepts about what causes bear attacks. A significant portion of bear incidents in parks can be attributed to unnatural attractants, habituated bears, and people making mistakes with bears.

In the last five years I have heard well over 150 stories about bear encounters from people who work in the woods. A totally different picture about bear aggressive behaviour emerges when this information is taken into consideration, and it parallels my own experiences with bears. Unfortunately, the government ministries in B.C. who should be generating good bear encounter information are handicapped by the biases that exist in some published data and by an unwillingness to obtain information from personnel at the bottom end of the government ministries who are taking most of the bear hazard risk.

There are very few biologists interested in studying bear aggressive behaviour, and fewer organizations interested in funding such studies. There is significant resistance by some biologists to consider what bear aggressive behaviour is really about. This is not a planned conspiracy by most bear biologists; it is an unspoken, underlying bias that some biologists have, and the manifestation of our political and biological priorities that are presently heavily weighted towards bear preservation.

There was an interesting paper submitted to the Bear-People Conflict Symposium held at Yellowknife, Northwest Territories in April of 1987 by Finnish biologist Erik S. Nyholm, who studied

brown bears (grizzlies) for 30 years. He stated in his
paper that there was a 42.8% increase in the frequency of bear attacks on humans between 1982 and
1986. He attributes this increase to a change in bear
behaviour (losing fear of people) which has resulted
from outright protection of bears in some areas.

This gentleman must have rural ties because his
views are different from most city biologists. He is
not making a statement about the difference between
protecting bears and not protecting them; he is taking a position about the difference between protecting
bears versus over-protecting them.

If Mr. Nyholm was a practicing biologist in B.C.
and tried to publish such a paper here, his career
would be finished in short order. His work would be
pounded into a pulp during peer-review, and there
would be no funding available for any future work of
this type. One must not make the mistake of thinking that the biological sciences actually move along
in an objective, neutral way. All bear studies have to
be funded and approved, and any such proposed study
in B.C. must past the litmus test of political correct-
ness, preservation, and value of political points.

In my opinion, we are slowly entering into a new
era in our relationship with bears. There will be
more bears in B.C. and much less negative-condi-
tioning influence by people on bear behaviour. This
will result in more human/bear conflict and in more
bear encounters that are hard to survive. Some bear
biologists would disagree with me on this subject, not
because of clear evidence to the contrary, but because
they fear that such a concept could be used to justify
the hunting and control killing of bears in order to
reduce bear danger to people.

I advocate that we should and must use hunting and
control killing of bears for reducing bear danger to
British Columbians. This concept has just about been
purged from bear management policies.

The information contained in this book comes from four main sources:

1. My own 29 years of experience in dealing with bold and aggressive bears and my years of extensive research into the evolutionary and genetic bases for mammalian behaviour.
2. Stephen Herrero's book *Bear Attacks* (1985).
3. Published bear research studies.
4. Information and stories obtained from Department of Fisheries and Oceans personnel, B.C. Parks personnel, Ministry of Forest personnel, Conservation Officers, safety officers, guides, trappers, hunters, and loggers.

2

Human/Bear
Conflict History

Human/bear conflict probably started about 100,000 years ago when our primitive ancestors fanned out across the Northern Hemispheres. At that time there were many large predators that humans had to deal with in order to survive. By about 13,000 years ago, the last glacial period had ended, and many predators and other types of animals had suffered extinction. In most northern regimes this left humans competing primarily with bears and wolves.

Human conflict with wild animals took on new meaning approximately 9,000 years ago when we took up farming and animal husbandry as our main means of survival. As human populations started increasing and expanding throughout Eurasia, bear populations started a long continuous decline and were eventually eliminated from vast areas of that continent around 2,000 years ago.

During the European exploration and settlement of North America there was considerable conflict between people and wild animals, and of course major conflict between Europeans and Native Americans. At that time in history the conquest of new lands and peoples was the priority, and nature was an enemy to be subdued. Both of these competing human cultures impacted the land, but European technology and weaponry was a thousand years more advanced, and by the middle of the 19th century, the North American continent had already been significantly altered.

In the late 1800s, after considerable destruction of most animal populations, a system of protecting wild animal species slowly evolved. If it had not been for some far-sighted individuals, like Theodore Roosevelt, grizzly bears south of the border would not now exist.

Between 1900 and about 1958 our culture, to a degree, still embraced a belief system about nature that was based on our right to exploit it as we saw fit. But during that period wildlife conservation became a sophisticated system of game management that was mainly designed and financed by hunters. Many parks and wilderness areas were established to protect wildlife and to create recreational areas for future generations.

During the 1960s, a new nature philosophy evolved which expounded the principle that we must reduce our impact on the environment. This much-needed principle was mainly pushed forward by newly-formed environmental groups. Whenever a major shift in cultural belief happens, there are usually many half-truths incorporated into the new belief system.

Two of the most erroneous beliefs about nature that came out of the early 1960s were the concepts that bears could sense human intentions (whether you had malice towards them or not), and that if you followed a set of encounter rules, bears would not hurt you. Unfortunately, these beliefs contributed to some of the terrible events that took place shortly thereafter.

On August 13th, 1967, in separate incidents, two young women were killed by grizzly bears in Glacier National Park. There had never been anyone killed by a grizzly in Glacier Park before. During

the next 13 years following the Glacier Park incidents, there was a significant increase in grizzly
attacks that killed or injured people, including bear
biologists and photographers. Most of these happened
in parks; some were predatory or carcass defense;
many were sows defending cubs.

All of these attacks were studied by experts, and the
following contributing factors were determined:
increased hiking activity in back country areas,
garbage habituation by grizzly bears, careless handling of foods, approaching too close to bears for
viewing or photography, and accidental close
encounters. I'm sure that all of these contributing
factors played important roles in these tragic deaths
and injuries, but there was another contributing factor that has never been more than cautiously alluded
to: Between 1960 and 1980, most Parks Services
introduced a more lenient approach to killing
aggressive bears than they had in the 1950s. This
trend continued until about eight years ago. There
have now been successful lawsuits against National
Parks pertaining to bear attacks, and most parks
have slowly returned to a more vigorous policy for
dealing with dangerous bears. Equally important
are new policies to quickly close trails and camp-
sites when a dangerous bear may be in the area.

From 1980 to the present, bear attacks on people have
continued to increase, but the types of attacks and
types of locations have changed, and once again
there have been reasons identified: growing human
activity in wild areas, habituation to garbage by
bears, carelessness with bears, and close encounters
with bears. All of these reasons are correct, but the
most important factor that influences whether an
encounter becomes an attack, or whether an attack
becomes a human death, has not been explored at all.

Beginning in the late 1960s, most field worker job
positions in government ministries and private
companies were filled with young university-

educated people who did not carry firearms for defense against bears. I know of at least three deaths caused by black bears in the mid-1980s that most likely would not have happened in the 1950s or early 1960s, because during that previous period most field employees working in high bear hazard areas were old-type bushmen who were armed and knew how to defend themselves.

Every year in B.C. there are many cases of people defending themselves with firearms against bears. Most of these attacks go unreported because many Ministry of Environment personnel take the position that if a bear attacks, the person involved has done something to cause the assault. This "blame the victim" response thus deters many people from reporting their bear encounters. It is unfortunate that the data that biologists use to decipher bear aggressive behaviour towards humans is missing this extremely important component.

An important question comes to mind: Have human/bear incidents been increasing, or are more encounters ending up as successful attacks because fewer people are defending themselves?

It is not desirable or possible for all B.C. field workers to carry firearms. I am merely pointing out an important factor related to human injury or death during a bear attack. But there are crews in many areas who should have the right to carry firearms for defense against bears. Presently, some people are being denied this right.

The following excerpts are from a four-page letter sent to me that details a series of bear encounters that happened to a forestry crew during a month of field work. All of the encounters seemed predacious in nature. The author of this letter requested that I keep his identity and the location of these incidents confidential:

. . .

We had a number of encounters with bears while working on this site. The first encounter occurred during our first week in the area. My co-worker (Jeff) and I were just about to sit down on a log to have a lunch break when Jeff noticed a somewhat large tan-colored furry animal cut across the old narrow skid trail that we were working near. The animal didn't appear the least bit concerned or interested in our existence during this brief encounter. We were slightly startled but resumed work activities as if nothing had happened.

That afternoon we were working in two groups of two and separated from our other co-workers by a few hundred metres. The forest we were working in was extremely dense giving us visibility of about 15 metres at best. Jeff and I were surveying in a new plot boundary when the next incident happened. We were on the last line, which we had cleared slightly for visibility purposes, and I was just about to stake in the final plot corner. I asked Jeff to bring the sledge hammer up, and when he arrived at my side we realized very suddenly that we were very close to our furry friend. The corner of the plot that we were standing at was near a grassy opening 5-10 metres away. The bear, giving us little or no warning, charged at us from behind a large downed log. He was probably about 30-40 metres away and I had just enough time to load up and immediately fire the primitive bear banger. The darn thing nearly blew my hand off from the vibration but succeeded in stopping the bear momentarily. We were expecting to see this probably now near-deaf bear turn and run like the wind, but instead it appeared to be preparing to approach even closer. After Jeff stomped out a small ground fire right beside where we were standing (obviously caused from the bear banger), we slowly backed away from the bear, proceeding down our plot line back to the other two guys to describe our experience.

No one in our group was armed with anything but a bear banger, so we decided to commence working in another area which was quite some distance from the bear and much closer to the pickup. After discussing the situation and knowing that we had to, at some time in the next couple of weeks, go back into the same area where the encounter occurred, we decided to talk to the Conservation Officer most experienced with that area about what to do in the case of another encounter.

Jeff and myself were thoroughly convinced that, due to the aggressive nature and the tan and dark brown two-tone markings of the bear, it had to be a grizzly. However, after we described everything to the Conservation Officer (C.O.) after work, he said that it was a large male cinnamon-colored black bear. He also warned us that some loggers in the area had also complained about a similar aggressive bear. For these reasons he recommended that if we had to go back to the area to work that we be armed with a defender shotgun loaded with five 12-gauge slugs for protection in case of another close aggressive encounter. He also asked that if the bear was shot that he be notified in a written report detailing the situation.

It turned out that one of the seasonal workers was an experienced and properly qualified hunter and he had a couple of shotguns sent up on the bus the next day so we could commence working with some sense of protection. Generally speaking, packing around firearms of any type would be greatly discouraged (by

management); however, this job was essential
for us to complete and we could not relocate the
research trial to another location. So, taking
the C.O.'s advice, we kept loaded shotguns
near our work area and continued with our job.

For the next 2-3 weeks we did not see hide nor
hair of any bears; we were even beginning to
wonder if packing these guns back and forth
from the trucks to the work area was even
warranted anymore. It was right about the
time when our guard was down, and we had all
but forgotten about the last bear incident, that
the next encounter occurred (Murphy's law, I
guess!). As in the previous incident we had
been working in separate teams, Jeff and I
again working together. All our plots that were
to be established in this research trial were now
in place, but prior to thinning the plots to their
required densities we had to complete these pre-
spacing density plots. This required going
into each established area and randomly locat-
ing four temporary plots. In these temporary
pre-density plots all of the trees are counted and
measured for diameter.

This is what Jeff and I were doing when the
next incident occurred. We had been in this
particular plot for quite some time, probably 20
minutes to 1/2 hr, and we were working on the
last of the four pre-density plots. This involves
one person measuring and relaying the data
back to the other person, who is recording the
data. So we actually make quite a bit of noise
while doing these type of plots, so much so that I
could vaguely make out the other guys doing
the same thing off in the distance somewhere
below us. While we were doing this work there
were brief moments when all was quiet, and it
was then that I noticed a light crack of some
small ground slash near us. I dropped down to

ground level in the direction of the noise, after telling Jeff, who was unaware of any impending danger, to keep quiet. It was then I realized that we were being sized up by another similar colored bear who was circling around us in tighter and tighter circles. When I told Jeff about the bear, it was only about 30-40 feet away and closing in slowly. It was very strange behaviour that I had never witnessed by any type of animal except by sharks on T.V. shows. When we yelled at this bear, it didn't even do anything to change its current behaviour. I began to feel that we were in real danger from this situation. I called down to Bill, the trained hunter, to come over to us and to bring his gun. Meanwhile, the bear just continued to circle us, getting increasingly closer.   When Bill arrived, he immediately took aim and shot the bear, which was now only about 20 feet away. The one shot that killed the bear actually knocked it right off its feet, but it somehow got up and ran about 40 feet, then died.

We were all in a state of shock when we went over to the bear to see what it looked like. We were surprised that this bear was about a 175 -200 lb female with a very poor looking coat of fur. We decided that we would have to relocate the carcass so that the danger of running into another bear would be lessened. We tied ropes around her front paws and with all four of us pulling, dragged her far away from where we were working. Bill wrote a report which he filed that evening with the C.O. We all felt bad that we ended this little bear's life, thinking, "gee maybe it was just curious or something." I don't feel that way now that I have attended your course; I am almost positive that she was stalking us down to be her next meal and had we not protected ourselves someone probably -

either Jeff or I - would have been seriously injured or even killed.

. . .

Jeff and I were convinced, however, that the first bear we had encountered was the real danger to us and was still out there somewhere. It appeared to us that the first bear was close to twice the size of the bear we shot and had a beautiful coat with somewhat lighter markings than did the female. Also, the report from the C.O., who told us that it was a 9-15-year-old male that was causing the problems out in this area, confirmed in my mind that the bear we shot was not the same bear we encountered in our first two incidents.

. . .

I personally would still be more comfortable with a firearm for protection than a bear spray. I think that employees like myself who are required to work in all areas of the province, and particularly areas with a high bear hazard, deserve the best possible protection. If the Ministry's excuse for not allowing firearms for protection is the lack of overall training and experience, then the proper training should be given to those affected employees.

Every year I am approached by 20-30 people who ask me to lobby on their behalf for the right to carry firearms for defense against bears. In light of the increase in predatory bear attacks, it is essential that people who work in bear habitat be allowed to carry firearms for self-defense.

In the last ten years there has been increasing interest by some government agencies and some biologists in improving their knowledge of how and why bear attacks happen. But this has been an unsuccessful game of catch-up because since the middle 1960s the frequency of different categories of attacks has been changing and is still changing, and each attack category requires a different defense strategy. Some of the bear safety pamphlets still being handed out have strategies that were relevant to the main type of bear attack taking place 20 years ago. Those strategies are extremely dangerous to use in relation to the most common type of attack (predatory black bear attacks) that is now taking place in many areas of North America.

I believe that the primary reason for the change in frequency of attack categories is human changes - changes in the way we approach nature and deal with bears. But there is time-lag between cause and effect, a lag in biologists' recognition of the changes, and an additional lag as to when bureaucracies start using the new biological information. Some of the most important bear attack information that came out of Herrero's book in 1985, is just now being incorporated into some government information - ten years too late.

For much of history humans considered bears as prime competitors and killed them at every opportunity. During the first half of the 19th century we slowly learned an appreciation of nature, but we still considered bears extremely dangerous animals. During the 1960s the pendulum swung too far the other way: Bears became cuddly little creatures that wouldn't hurt you unless you did something to deserve it. We slowly worked our way towards a more realistic synthesis of the two views during the 1980s, but we still haven't reached an accurate view of reality. I hope this book will help us get there.

3

Bear Biology

North America has three of the world's eight species of bears: polar, grizzly, and black. Most of the other species in other parts of the world are seriously threatened, and some may not survive the next 20 years. The ancestral stock for bears did not originate in North America, and like many other animals and all humans, they are recent immigrants.

Although the grizzly bear's original range of distribution has been significantly reduced, all three North American bears are presently surviving quite well. That optimistic statement would have been hard to make 20 years ago, but through the efforts of many dedicated people, we are now much more successful at protecting bear populations. However, the long-term view is more pessimistic: If human population growth continues at the present rate, grizzlies may not survive beyond the middle of the next century.

All North American bears are related, and evolved from a more carnivorous ancestor. Grizzly bears and black bears probably speciated from each other about three million years ago. Both evolved towards omnivorism and presently survive on a wide range of food types; both are primarily vegetarian; both still possess remnant predatory behaviour. Polar bears probably speciated from grizzly bears no longer than 100,000 years ago and have evolved back to carnivorism. Polar bears and grizzlies are sibling species, and fertile offspring have resulted in zoo matings between the two.

There are similarities and differences in the characteristics of these species. We must explore these attributes if we are to understand what makes each of them unique.

DIFFERENCES IN NORTH AMERICAN BEARS

Polar bears have a circumpolar distribution in the Arctic and spend a good portion of their lives on the sea ice hunting seals. During the summer, when the ocean ice breaks up, they go inland and eat a variety of foods. They are almost always white or yellowish in color and they are the largest of the bear species, with some large males weighing over 1,200 pounds (I will use imperial weights in this section as most people relate their own weight and the weight of animals to this system). This species was overhunted in the past, but is now well protected.

Grizzly bears are considered a sub-species of the Eurasian Brown Bear which they have been isolated from for about 10,000 years. There is considerable confusion over different regional names for this species. On the coast of Alaska they are referred to as kodiaks or browns. Inland Alaskans usually call these bears grizzlies. In Canada and the continental U.S. they are also called grizzlies.

Grizzly distribution reaches from Northwestern Alaska to northern Montana and Idaho. This population is one gene pool, so I consider it one species with local races. There is also a genetically isolated remnant race of grizzly in the Yellowstone Park area.

Grizzlies can be large animals with the males of some races approaching 1,200 pounds. On the coast of B.C. mature males average 650-800 lbs, and rare ones occasionally tip the scales at 1,000 lbs. Females are generally about 30% smaller.

The main grizzly diet is vegetation, but bears can digest a wide variety of foods. Their digestive system, body design, and behaviour all show signs of having evolved from predator to omnivore. Their percentage of vegetable matter intake varies from 65%-90% of their total diet depending on location. This species has developed a pattern of foraging in both alpine and forested regions. They have a claw design and shoulder hump muscles for digging and accessing roots. They also do a considerable amount of digging for ground-burrowing mammals.

Grizzly bear anatomical features are usually distinguishable (but not always) from black bears by their shoulder hump, dished face, longer claws, and lower head carriage. When they are walking at a normal pace, their backs do not have the general straight appearance of the black bear. A grizzly has a slightly forward sloping back, a shoulder hump, and a drop to the head. This low head carriage gives more swagger to the their walk.

Grizzlies generally come in shades of blond, brown, or black. Most bears have a mix of these colors and are usually lighter in the head and shoulder areas, or with lighter tipping of some hair. Some will have a light band just behind the shoulders, especially when young. They generally turn darker as they get older, and males are often darker in some populations.

Black bears are closely related to the Asiatic black bear and probably also related to the sun bear, spectacled bear, and sloth bear. Black bears range over a large portion of North America and have been the most successful bear at adapting to man. They are, in general, not threatened.

Their size varies greatly by race. On the B.C. coast black bears are a smaller variety with males rarely

going over 400 lbs. In other areas males can go over
600 lbs; trophy records indicate that large black
bears can come from many different areas of North
America.

Their diet is much like the grizzly bear's, but the
black bear has evolved as a forest animal and has
evolved a sharp, hooked claw for tree climbing
defense. They compete with grizzlies for vegetation
and fish in some ecosystems but do not have the digging ability to substantially utilize underground
food. They are successful predators of moose calves
and other animals in some areas.

A black bears' ears are longer and more pointed
than a grizzly's. They also have a straight or
"roman-nose" face profile and higher head carriage
when walking. They are generally black in color
but also come in varying shades of brown. Most, but
not all, have a white patch (sometimes shaped like a
V) on their chest. The kermode bear on the B.C.
North Coast is a white-phase black bear.

One common confusion I hear is people referring to
light brown or blond black bears as cinnamon bears,
and other people think they are talking about grizzlies. Cinnamon bears are black bears, not grizzlies.

MATING, GESTATION, AND CUBS

Bears mate in early summer and stay with each
other for a week or longer. If bear population density
is high, bears of both genders may breed with more
than one mate. They do not mate for life.

Female bears have evolved a unique ability to sus-
pend the growth of the fertilized egg when it reaches
the stage called blastocist. The egg sits in a suspended state and does not attach to the uterine wall
until late fall. A gestation period of about three
months then follows, and cubs are born in January
or February when the sow is in her den.

Grizzly cubs usually stay with their mothers for two

years after coming out of the den the first year. Occasionally the cubs are with their mother for three years as breeding intervals vary and, in most populations, average between three and four years. Black bear cubs usually only get the sow's mothering for one and a half years, and they are very vulnerable during their first year on their own.

COMMUNICATION

Bears communicate to each other and to other species with a range of visual and auditory signals. These signals are important in reducing tension amongst bears, warning intruders to back off, displaying sexual interest, and providing other information.

Because bears are mostly solitary and aggressive animals, much of their communication is threat or appeasement in nature. Sometimes the first warning signals of potential violent action are subtle, and it takes a seasoned bear watcher to recognize them.

(Bear *communication* information will be spread throughout this book in context to bear encounters.)

BEAR MARK TREES

Bears also have an important communicative system of marking trees in peculiar ways. I have spent years observing bear marking sign and it's obvious that it parallels the "signing" of other animal species. Wolves, cougars, coyotes, foxes, and many other animals have sign posts that help communicate location, hierarchy status, gender, mating receptivity, etc.

Bears sometimes rub trees to relieve itching, but they will also rub to leave a scent. They sometimes rear up side-ways to a tree, stretch out, and bite the tree with two canine teeth as high as they can reach. I call this hierarchy marking. Sometimes bears rub

Hierarchy tree, Atnarko River, B.C.   *Gary Shelton*

their scent on a tree, then walk away twisting their
feet with each step.

The most fascinating marking behaviour I have
observed is what I call forward facing marking. I

Rub tree, Big Creek, B.C. *Gary Shelton*

believe it is only done by dominant male grizzlies prior to and during breeding season. It is only done on particular types of trees - usually large, preferably fir. As the bear approaches the tree, but is still

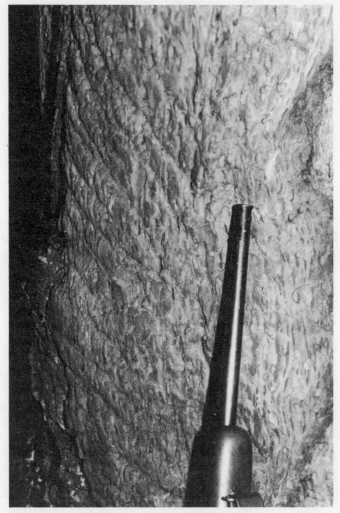

Forward facing mark tree, Talchako River, B.C.

Gary Shelton

about six metres away, it starts sliding its front feet back and forth and swinging its head side to side, and slowly moving forward. When it reaches the tree, it stands up facing the tree, reaches high with its front claws, and creates a series of scratches in the bark of the tree from top to bottom. It then walks away from the tree, sliding and swinging, about six metres, then turns around and repeats the performance two or three times. The well-spaced holes that are left in the ground from this behaviour can be

Even baby bears mark trees.   *courtesy Stefan Himmer*

six inches deep, but look similar to the more shallow bears-stepping-in-the-same-place type of traffic wear.

Some of these mark tree and step-hole features could

be 500 years old or older. I once found barely dec-
ernable slide-hole features that were extremely old,
without a mark tree, but upon careful examination
the artifact of an ancient fir mark tree that had died
and fallen over a half century earlier was still
there.

Bears will mark any changes in the environment
that they come across. On many occasions I have
seen where they did this with temporary fire camps,
hunting camps, logging slashes, or a new cabin.
They mark these kinds of environmental changes
within the first couple of years of disturbance.

HIBERNATION

About 15 years ago a biologist who was studying
denning bears stated in a publication that bears are
not true hibernators. Unfortunately, he didn't qual-
ify his statement with a secondary phrase, "in relation to metabolism." If one studies bear evolution,
bear physiology, and bear behaviour, it becomes
obvious that bears are true hibernators according to
the definition in most dictionaries. This misunder-
standing caused a de-emphasis of the importance of
bear denning behaviour.

Bear hibernation has evolved as an important
omnivoristic strategy: It suspends the need for food
intake when types of vegetation that they can digest
are not available. Bears cannot break down cellu-
lose like ungulates, nor can they digest low-value
dead winter plants. In northern climates bears must
eat all summer in order to sleep all winter.

Grizzlies usually dig their dens at elevations
between 800-1,700 metres. Black bears generally
den lower at 400-1,000 metres, sometimes digging
their dens but often using hollow trees or other natural features. Both species build mattresses in their
dens using boughs or other plant materials.

After a bear becomes an adult, it usually dens in the

It took my hunting partners and I four years of backtrack-ing in spring snow to locate the above pictured den. We monitored this den for five years. The large male tore out and replaced the hemlock bough mattress each of the first three years, then slept on bare ground the next two years. Within 100 metres of the den there were three old collapsed dens, and five attempted digs where he came up against solid rock. He now has a new den about 75 metres up the hill side. (Above: Randy Svisdahl)   *Gary Shelton*

same area for long periods of its life. Bears are secretive about their den sites, and will change den-ning location if seriously disturbed.

Black bear dens on the mid coast of B.C. are often found in hollow cedar trees, or dug under the root mass of a fallen tree, or dug under a pile of large woody debris. I saw one den dug under a large flat rock.

Because grizzlies den at higher elevations, logging and other human activities usually do not affect their den sites. However, logging often does disturb black bear denning areas; what negative effects this may have is not yet known.

Common type black bear den dug underneath root mass of fallen tree. Den entrance is on right side of bottom picture just behind roots. *Gary Shelton*

The amount of time that a bear spends in its den each winter depends on weather, and bears may be out and active during winter mild spells.

YEARLY BEHAVIOUR

Both black and grizzly bears come out of their dens between April 1st and May 15th, some years even earlier. Some of these bears move down to a lower elevation and feed along rivers, tide flats, lake shores, swamps, meadows, and low elevation burns. Others stay up high and feed in avalanche chutes and slide areas. They are after a variety of plants that are just starting growth: grasses, sedge, clover, horsetail, peavine, fiddlehead fern, etc.

In the middle of May, breeding activity starts and lasts for about seven weeks. After breeding is over, grizzlies spread throughout the whole ecosystem including alpine areas. In most areas, black bears utilize low elevation and hill-side habitat through the summer. In July, August, and September, berries, insects, and small mammals become important foods and bears are usually found in open-canopy-forests, riparian zone areas, burns, logging slashes, and hill-side slide areas.

In many locations, bears go after salmon in the fall. In places without fish, bears generally maintain their summer regimen and sometimes move to higher elevations. Black bears rarely venture above tree line in habitats where they co-exist with grizzlies. Both locate their den sites in late fall and then den up when the first major winter snow storm hits. Cubs of both species are born in January - February, and when they come out in the spring with their mothers, the yearly process of survival starts anew.

4

Bear Aggressive Behaviour

It is a very powerful writing device to compare two species in order to explore their similarities and differences. If you try to extend this principle to three species, though, the material becomes a confusing mass of information.

Polar bear aggression, encounters, defense strategy, and the circumstances of the environment they live in, require different explanations. Therefore, I have written a separate later chapter for polar bears. This chapter, and following chapters, pertain to grizzlies and black bears only.

Bear aggressive behaviour is very complex and difficult to understand, and much of it is still unknown. But what is known about both black bear and grizzly bear behaviour sheds considerable light on what occurs during a bear encounter. There are, however, significant differences in behaviour between these two species, and it is impossible to understand these differences without an evolutionary perspective of how they arrived at their present state.

Grizzly bears evolved over a long period of time in open habitat conditions during the Pleistocene Epoch, with many extremely dangerous megafauna predators. Grizzlies developed a defensive-aggressive behavioural mode of challenging intruders by ferocious bluffing and, if necessary, making contact with and immobilizing the threat, then quickly retreating. Sow grizzlies usually defend their young by having them run in the opposite direction of the threat (if the danger can be clearly located); then the sow exhibits bluffing displays and either makes contact with the intruder or runs off after the cubs. Whether a grizzly makes contact in this situation depends on several factors:

1. The aggressiveness of the particular bear.
2. What events have just preceded the encounter.
3. The distance to the threat and, in the case of a sow with cubs, whether or not the distance between the intruder and the cubs is being increased.

In the present evolutionary period, grizzlies do not have any formidable competitive predators that threaten their safety, except humans. But for eons they co-existed and inter-reacted with a host of dangerous animals with no way of escaping from them except through ferocious behaviour. Even though the megafauna predators of the past who influenced grizzly bear behaviour have become extinct in the last 13,000 years, grizzly behavioural patterns will continue for thousands of years into the future.

Grizzlies do not have the ability to determine whether or not people actually pose a threat to them. Their aggressive-defensive behaviour does not work that way; if it did, they would have probably suffered extinction a long time ago. A reactive system that employs a quick aggressive response to any intrusion has given grizzlies a survival edge against other competitive species.

Occasional variations on this grizzly bear open-habitat aggressive-defensive behaviour do occur, and they usually lead to very dangerous situations, which I will explain later.

Black bears developed a behavioural pattern of living in forested areas and using trees for defense early in their evolutionary development. In general, black bears are less aggressive than grizzlies but are equally dangerous because of their more predatory nature towards people. They will make the same bluffing displays as grizzlies when threatened but are less likely to make contact. Sows usually defend their cubs by sending them up a tree, then they stand at the base of the tree making bluffing displays towards the perceived threat. If a single bear or a sow cannot dissuade an intruder by bluffing, it will sometimes make contact, but more often it will also go up a tree.

Predacious black bear behaviour is different. Usually a predacious bear does not show any anger or bluffing. It follows its prey in a stalking mode, often circling and moving closer. If it decides the prey is takeable the bear charges, takes the prey down, then kills and eats it. Black bears are more difficult to read during encounters because they are not as "upfront" as grizzlies are in letting humans know their intentions. They can be very unpredictable, so be alert for signs of predacious behaviour.

TYPES OF BEAR AGGRESSIVE BEHAVIOUR

Most species' populations are held in check by food availability, predation, and parasitism. Some animals at the top of the food chain have another limiting factor: intraspecies strife and competition. Bear population regulation seems to be influenced mainly by food availability and intraspecies mortality. To quote a statement from the *Grizzly Bear Compendium* (1987), under Population Regulation, "Thus, density-independent (nutritional regulation) and density-dependent (social) mechanisms appear to be implicated in bear population regulation."

Nutritional regulation of a population would primarily cause sows to sexually mature later, breed less often, and to have smaller litters. Social regulation would be manifest primarily in aggressive behaviours that cause mortality - dominant males killing cubs, sub-adult males, and sometimes complete families. It would also cause death in competitive battles over breeding and indirectly cause death of bears who are out-competed for food resources.

In reality, the two mechanisms of bear population regulation, nutritional and social, are an interwoven complex of aggression, competition, and available nutrition.

A significant part of bear aggressive behaviour is related to density-dependant (social) population regulation.   This mechanism, and its associated aggressive behaviours, exists in all bear populations and can become acute when high population densities occur. The following types of bear aggression, with the exception of predatory aggression, do not only pertain to population regulation but also to genetic selectivity.

(See Note #1 at the end of this chapter about the following types of bear aggressive behaviour.)

There are five general types of bear aggression:

1.   Predatory   (including carcass defense).
2.   General competitiveness (including breeding aggression).
3.   Home range.
4.   Male cub-killing.
5.   Female cub defense.

1. Predatory aggression: Both black bears and grizzlies have a degree of predacious instinct, but this instinct is manifest in somewhat different

ways. Herrero's studies brought out an important
point in relation to attack categories: Most serious
injuries and deaths caused by black bears are predatory in nature; that is, the bear is trying to kill the
person for food. Statistics indicate that black bears
are more predacious towards humans than are grizzlies. Grizzly bears do occasionally kill people for
food, but most serious injuries and deaths caused by
grizzlies, excluding park attacks, are defensive-
aggressive in nature.

An interesting statistical observation about predacious attacks by both species is that most people killed
by a predatory grizzly are people camping in a park
at night. Most people killed by predacious black
bears are people doing various types of activities during the day, and are sometimes children. Predatory
black bears often take time to carefully assess potential prey. It is my opinion that if humans were only
half the size we are, we would have major problems
with black bears. Be very careful with your
children.

Bears do not have a refined prey profile in relation
to predatory behaviour like most true predators. For
example, if a bear was lying on a hill-side and saw a
bull moose walk by, it would most likely pay little
attention. If, on the other hand, a cow moose with a
small calf walked by, a predatory interest would be
triggered in most bears upon seeing the small calf.
The sight of an animal that appeared to be injured
would also trigger a predatory interest in most bears.
The appearance of vulnerability, and the thought of a
significant reward for little effort with little chance
of injury, probably play key roles in many predatory
attacks.

What about everything else that falls in between a
bull moose and a calf moose, and what goes through a
bear's mind when it sees a human? It is next to
impossible to accurately define predation in bears
because it is a remnant behaviour, and each bear's

genetic makeup, learned behaviour, and level of hunger at a given time can vary.

Grizzlies and black bears have been evolving towards omnivorism for a long time and must devote most of their time securing plant foods as a basic survival strategy. But animal tissue has a significantly higher food value than plant foods, and even though bears could not now in general survive over the long haul as true predators, some types of circumstances will bring their predatory behaviour forward. Something as simple as encountering a human who is lying on the ground may trigger a predatory response, especially if the bear is very hungry. That same person in a standing position would probably not look takeable. If dealing with an African Lion, on the other hand, it wouldn't matter whether a person was lying or standing; the person would fit into the lion's prey profile.

Many grizzlies that attack predaciously are habituated to human garbage, but most black bears that act as a predator towards humans are wild or only slightly habituated to human presence. A good portion of the predacious black bear encounters I have heard about in the last few years, where the bear was killed, have involved three-year-old males. These young bears were probably under considerable competitive stress and very hungry.

My own studies indicate that there has been a significant and little-known shift during the last nine years in the frequency and category of victims of predacious black bear attacks. Predacious black bear attacks are by far the most dangerous type of attack in B.C., and the majority of victims are people who are working in the field during the day. If this seems hard to believe, consider the following statistics obtained from the Wildlife Branch: Between 1984 and 1992 there were 25 people injured and five people killed by black bears in B.C. Most of the black bear attacks were predatory in nature. In the same time period, there were only four injuries and one death caused by grizzlies.

Most predators have developed aggressive behaviour for defending a carcass that they have killed or found. Some African predators, for example, have more difficulty defending a carcass than killing the animal. This behaviour in bears is dangerous for people, especially in the case of grizzly bears.

It is important to have a clear understanding of predacious behaviour. Carefully read the stories in the *Predacious Encounters and Attacks* chapter.

2. General competitiveness aggression: Bears must compete against each other for food, cover, dens, breeding privileges, etc. Each bear must try to jockey its way up the hierarchy so that it can spend more time eating than running away. Hibernation intensifies the competition because bears must obtain their yearly food requirement in six to eight months.

Bears are generally antagonistic toward each other, with a lot of huffing-puffing and threat displays being the norm during encounters. These sometimes end in fights and occasionally death. However, bears have evolved a complicated system of threat and appeasement signals that reduce potential danger to both parties.

During spring breeding, males become quite aggressive toward other breeding males, sub-adult males (three to five years), and probably toward females with cubs who are not identifiable by smell.

This general competitive aggression does cause mortality, mainly for males who are competing for females and dominance. Once a bear is six years or older, it has a good chance of living to be over 20.

3. Home range aggression: Bears are not exclusively territorial; they are semi-territorial - that is, their home ranges overlap and they will use and defend high-value areas according to their position in the hierarchy of power. These home ranges vary in size from 150 sq km to 1,200 sq km, depending on the species, sex, and age of the bear. Bears establish their home ranges in the first three years of being on their own, with females usually staying in the vicinity of their mother's home range and males moving to other areas (out-migration). Sows are sometimes quite tolerant of their female offspring but not of their male offspring.

In the fall of 1988, when I was guiding two moose hunters in the Cariboo Mountains, we repeatedly saw a larger grizzly moving around through a burn, followed at about four hundred metres by a smaller grizzly. Day after day, while we were looking for moose, we would see this pair, but they never came close to each other. The hunters were intrigued by this behaviour and wanted an explanation. I told them that the smaller bear was a third-year female cub who was still yearning for her mother, but the sow had set the limit of tolerance at about 400 metres. The sow would probably give birth the following spring, and the cub would eventually stop following her.

There was also a female with a first-year cub and a large male that we occasionally saw. These grizzlies, and probably others that we did not see, all had overlapping home ranges in the burn where we were hunting. We, of course, saw many black bears as well; all these bears were there for the wealth of blueberries.

When young bears are establishing their home ranges, they are subjected to a considerable amount of aggression from other bears. They sometimes receive fatal injuries during encounters. Quite often they are denied access to high-value food areas. This in turn can reduce food intake, particularly if the population density is high. If a bear has not built up sufficient fat reserves by denning time, it does not survive the winter.

4. Male cub-killing aggression: This behaviour is common throughout nature. In those species that have been carefully studied, the results are usually the same: males are killing the offspring of other males. However, the way in which this behaviour is manifest varies greatly, and in many species is rather bizarre. In some species the infanticidal males cannot identify their own offspring, but can identify females that they have bred with recently. It is still unclear what this behaviour means in bears, but there have been many observations of its existence, and it is probably most prevalent during spring breeding season when males are more aggressive.

Sometimes a male will kill both the sow and cubs. Large males also inflict significant mortality on sub-adult males. One strange aspect of this behaviour, only with grizzlies, is that on some occasions the killing male will only partially cannibalize the carcass of his victim. We saw this behaviour in the spring of 1992 when one of our collared males killed a younger collared male. Both were part of the Atnarko South Tweedsmuir Park Grizzly Study. (I sit on the committee that oversees this study.) The older male consumed only about a quarter of the remains.

The most important aspect of this behaviour is the reactive behaviour of females in defense of their cubs, and the overall effect on total bear aggressiveness within a population.

I have been aware of male cub-killing behaviour for over 20 years (see the last story in the *Attacks, Encounters, and Incidents* chapter). When I first expressed views on this subject between 1973 and 1975, I came up against a brick wall. At that time, our culture believed that only humans killed their own kind, and my views were unacceptable. In the last six to eight years most of the bear biology community have come accept the existence of this behaviour.

(See Note #2 at the end of this chapter.)

5. Cub defense aggression: The ferocity of female bears defending their young (particularly grizzlies) is legendary, and there is good reason for it. The ferocity and willingness to suffer injury or death gives a sow bear the ability (in most cases) to defend her cubs against a male that may be twice her size. This is also an important behaviour in defense against individuals of other species.

When a sow grizzly is standing in open ground and must defend her cubs against a dangerous opponent, she must convince the intruder that even though she may lose the battle, she will inflict significant damage. Cub defense behaviour is explosive, seems to be genetically programmed, and is probably chemically induced. I have seen sow bears trigger into this response and not de-trigger until the acceptable distance between the cubs and me was achieved. This behaviour does not necessarily mean that contact will be made because much of it is designed to scare the hell out of what it is being directed at, and it usually does. In some cases, the sow will show restraint if contact is made, inflicting only minor damage, then quickly retreating. In other cases, the perceived threat may lose an eye, ear, nose, and a good portion of the scalp in the first few seconds.

Over the years I have had many encounters with sow grizzlies with cubs. When I was young and foolish I enjoyed them, but no more. I want to tell you something very important regarding all of those documentaries about bears that were filmed in Alaska, the ones that show fisherman or photographers on the Brooks River or at McNeil River Falls standing within a few metres of sows with cubs: Those bears are habituated to human presence. In those locations it took bears ten years or more to develop a learned tolerance of close human presence, but equally important is the open visual space and abundance of fish. Don't come to a river in the mid coast rain forest of B.C. and try to approach a sow grizzly with cubs

as shown in those films, or you might learn about cub
defense behaviour the hard way. (See the *Bear
Encounters* chapter for further information on grizzly family encounters and variations.)

An interesting side-note on cub defense behaviour
is the fact that within a week after a sow grizzly
comes into estrus, during May of the second or third
year after giving birth, she no longer cares whether
her cubs live or die. This is a terrible time for the
cubs, as mother's doting care is replaced with a
smack on the snout every time they try to approach
her.

I saw an example of this in May of 1984 when a
friend of mine shot a grizzly in an area where grizzlies were re-establishing mark trees along the edge
of a logging slash. When my friend started to skin
out the bear, he became aware that he was surrounded
by grizzlies who were moving back and forth nearby. One bear approached him and would not back
off. He quickly left the area and came and asked my
son Tyler and me to help him out of his predicament.

When we arrived on the scene it took me a little
while to figure out what was going on. A sow with
three third-year cubs was in estrus and being pursued by two males, one of which had been shot by my
friend. The cubs were intermixing with three, then
two, adult bears who were indifferent to the cubs' survival. The cubs were going up and down small fir
trees like yo-yos in order to avoid being mauled.
The other larger male stayed out of our sight, but his
tracks were obvious.

My friend and my son stood on each side of me,
yelling at these bears as I skinned out the dead bear.
Several times I had to stop skinning and throw large
limbs at one or the other of the cubs to get them to stop
approaching us. It was a nerve-racking situation,
especially because we didn't want to kill any more
bears.

It is extremely important that you understand the

types of bear aggressive behaviour described above
because certain aspects of these can be directed toward humans. These behaviours are not omnipres-
ent in most bear populations, but they are always
there in the background causing some bear mortality; they mainly come into play when population levels approach the inter-reactive social maximum.

Bears can also display tolerance of each other, particularly toward near relatives, long-term acquain-
tances, and in general towards most other bears
when there is an abundance of food. Even though
their demeanour is usually serious, they can be very
inquisitive and often playful. I'll never forget
watching two first-year grizzly cubs observing and
trying to mimic their mother's fishing technique.
They would take turns walking out on a medium-
sized log that hung about a foot above a river side-
channel pool like a springboard. At the end of the log
they would hesitate for about ten seconds, then dive in
and romp about, splashing water all over their
mother, not quite sure what they were looking for.
They were enjoying their play, but every once in a
while they would catch a glimpse of large salmon
whizzing by their legs, and go tearing back to mom
while looking back over a shoulder like they had just
seen the devil. I have spent many enjoyable hours of
quiet laughter watching bear antics and play.

HOME RANGE AGGRESSION TOWARDS PEOPLE

The types of bear aggressive behaviour that mainly
concern us are predatory, home range, and cub
defense. Predatory and cub defense behaviours
towards people are explained in their sections, but in
the *Home Range Aggression* section of this chapter, I
describe only the aspects of this behaviour that relate
to *bear/bear* conflict. The way in which this aggressive behaviour can be directed towards humans is

very complex and deserves special, separate attention here.

General competitive aggression and dominant male cub-killing aggression are mainly about bear-to-bear interaction: establishing hierarchy, breeding aggression, and lethal elimination of competition; those actions that happen in time, but are not related to space, and are primarily gene selective in nature. Home range aggression, on the other hand, has to do with defending particular high-value space - food, beds, dens - and is mainly population regulatory in nature.

When a bear has decided to make contact with an intruder, it stops using threat signals. But the threat-and-appeasement signals that bears have evolved to reduce actual combat are the compromise mechanism of their territorial home range aggression. These gestures are a warning to not come closer, or a warning that you are already too close and had better back up quickly. Young bears must quickly learn and refine the complex give-and-take aspect of their home range aggression if they are to survive and prosper.

If you were travelling along a highway in the springtime, and stopped to photograph a black bear who was eating grass along the side of the road, you would probably see home range aggression. If you were to approach within about 75 metres or so of the bear, you would probably see one or maybe all of the first signals of threat display: dropping the head, turning sideways, or turning to face you with a direct stare. The bear may then stomp its front feet, blow, growl, pop its teeth, or swat the ground. You would be close enough that the bear would feel your presence as a threat. The bear would be in a fight-or-flight state of mind, but the grass it is eating may be the only high-value food presently in its home range that is not dominated by a more powerful bear. It may prefer to stay right where it is.

If you were a foolish person and went closer for a better camera shot, you would probably see the bear's ears go flat and its spinal hair stand on end. It may then turn to a 45 degree angle to you, go stiff-legged, and bounce several times towards you, giving blowing or growling sounds with each bounce. It would then come to a facing halt, and watch your reaction. At this point even foolish people usually back off.

These threat display signals can be directed at other bears, other animals, and humans. They are of such a nature that most creatures can clearly decipher the message. But if the message-receiver does not show an appropriate response, like backing away quickly, a direct frontal charge may result with possible contact being made. There are occasionally human deaths related to this type of aggression with black bears, but home range aggression is the primary type of behaviour involved in most minor injuries inflicted by black bears.

This type of aggression includes all of those cases where bears place high value on human foods or garbage within their home ranges. A habituated bear usually does not give threat displays as it approaches people for food, but it will if it is met with resistance.

Grizzly bear home range aggression is a different ballgame. Grizzlies are much more aggressive than black bears in defending high-value space. Their aggressive displays, when defending an area of value, are almost identical to black bear threat signals, but they are usually much more determined to stay put, and the chance of contact is much greater.

Grizzly home range aggression is something that people must clearly understand and respect. Grizzlies have evolved a behavioural pattern of not easily being moved away from something they need. The survival of individual grizzlies, and the survival of the grizzly bear species, has depended on this important behavioural adaptation for a very long time.

Up until now, I have been categorizing bear attacks

strictly in relation to particular types of bear aggressive behaviour. Herrero identified attacks in his
book using different criteria than I do, and he
emphasized the danger of surprise close-range
encounters with grizzlies that he calls "sudden
encounters". When a person surprises a bear at
close range, the level of aggression is intensified, no
matter what behavioural pattern is involved. With a
grizzly bear, it may easily end up deadly.

In most attacks where a single grizzly kills or seriously injures someone, and where the bear was not
acting as a predator, surprise and close proximity
are the usual key factors. As a bear gets older and
more powerful, its home range aggression is
expressed as a general intolerance towards other
creatures who invade the *required defense re-action
zone*. This zone may have a radius as short as 25
metres for some young black bears, or may be as far
as 250 metres for some sow grizzlies that live in
alpine habitat.

If a bear catches another bear off guard and initiates
an attack, the other bear is momentarily at a significant disadvantage. This creates a situation where
the best defense for a bear in a surprise encounter
may be a swift aggressive response. This is not
some absolute behaviour in grizzly bears, and there
are many factors that influence a particular bear's
response in a given situation, but they will often
react violently towards a close-range intruder.

Again, I must make this important point: In general, grizzly bears cannot distinguish the level of
danger an intruder poses. Under some circumstances they will come after you with the same determined ferocity that they used for eons against the
likes of the saber-toothed cat, the North American
lion, the dire wolf, and the short-faced bear. They do
not know whether you want to end their life or wish
them well.

When a person surprises a grizzly bear at close

range and it rips and tears them apart, then quickly retreats, it is acting out the enforcement aspect of its home range aggression. Bears pack their exclusive territory around with them; it is a varying, invisible, elastic space they don't want trespassed.

* * *

Note #1.

The following is a qualification of the bear aggressive behaviour explained in this chapter.

If you examine the biological literature on bear behaviour you will find that biologists have studied bear attacks, bear aggressive interactions at feeding aggregations, and threat display signalling. You will also find many anecdotal pieces of information about bear aggression that have been observed by researchers doing other types of studies. No one has ever developed a definitive description of what the various types of bear aggression are about.

The information about bear aggression in this chapter - as I have categorized it, defined it, and inter related it - is unknown to biology. It is based on years of direct observations and extensive research into the evolutionary and genetic bases for mammalian behaviour. It has served me well, and it can serve you well, as an important basic guide to understanding what bear aggressive behaviour is all about. Without it I could not have written this book.

* * *

Note #2.

Peter Clarkson is the wolf-grizzly biologist for the Department of Renewable Resources, Government of Northwest Territories at Inuvik, N.W.T.

This gentleman has done considerable research into grizzly bear biology. He conducted a study of grizzly bears in the Anderson and Horton River areas of the Northwest Territories during the late 1980s and early 1990s. He was assisted by wolf-grizzly technician Ilme Liepins.

The purpose of the study was to determine population estimates for setting the allowable hunting harvest quota, and to obtain information about other aspects of bear biology.

The following is an excerpt from the June 1989 update of that study and pertains to natural mortality:

4.7.1 Natural Mortality

The natural mortality of radio-collared grizzly bears and their associate cubs was monitored in 1988-89. During capture work in early June 1988, three radio-collared females (G63, G65, G67) were found dead. A site investigation indicated that all three had been killed by another bear (presumably a large adult male).

G63 was found on a south facing slope of a small creek valley. The site had signs of a previous fight (broken branches, trampled bushes and grasses). G63 was about 90% consumed, however, large tooth puncture marks were visible in several places on the hide. G63 had been killed about 10-14 days before she was located. Large bear scats were found at the site indicating a large bear had been feeding on her. It was not possible to determine if she had cubs, however, she did not have cubs and was in breeding condition when captured in 1987. At the site there were three spruce trees (10-12 cm in diameter) that had been recently chewed off at about 2 m. It is possible that G63 had three Cubs Of the Year (C.O.Y) that were treed and killed by a large adult male after he had killed G63. The male would have chewed off the trees to capture the cubs. The above is only speculation based on the site investigation and cannot be verified.

G65 was killed at her den site, but not eaten. A field necropsy of G65 showed large tooth and scratch marks on her head, chest, and body. She had been dead 7-10 days before being found. The opening of the den had been torn apart and the den bedding material pulled out of the den. Small cub bones were found near the den. It was impossible to determine with certainty how many cubs she had, but judging from the bones found at the site there was a minimum of two cubs.

G67 and her three C.O.Y. were out of their den and had been located two times (28 May, 2 June 1988). While searching for bears the Supercub team spotted a large male eating G67 (4 June 1988). The helicopter team was called and captured the male (G128). A site investigation showed that there had been a major fight and G67 had bite marks on her head, neck, and body. The three cubs had been eaten and were found in fresh bear scats at the site. G67 was about 10% consumed. G128 did not have any visible injuries from the fight with G67. G128 weighed 209 kg when captured and appeared to be in good condition.

All three bears, G63, G65, and G67 were killed in close proximity to each other. It is not possible to determine if all three were killed by G128, however, the timing of the kills (G63: 10-14 days, G65: 7-10 days, G67: 1-2 days) would have allowed one bear to do the killing.

G69 was located with two C.O.Y. in early June, but was located alone on and after 9 June 1988. The cause of cub death could not be determined, however the cubs were lost during the breeding season and it is possible an adult male may have killed the cubs.

G79 and three C.O.Y. were captured in 1987.

All monitoring flights in 1988 showed that only two yearlings were with her. She had lost one cub during their first year.

G87, a two-year-old female, was with her mother G86 for most of May and early June. On 9 June 1988, G87 was located alone on the east shore of the Horton River and G86 was with an adult male approximately 8 km to the west. On 14 July 1988, G87 was found dead in the same area as her previous location. The cause of death could not be determined, however analysis of her skull showed a puncture which may have been caused by a large canine tooth.

Author's note: The above information really demonstrates the violent aggression that can be associated with density-dependant population regulatory control mechanisms and genetic selectivity. All animal species produce more offspring than can be assimilated into the population. In some predators, the killing of one's own kind is the main regulatory mechanism. In prey species, nutrition, predation, and parasitism are the controlling factors.

It is quite possible to regulate bear hunting in a way that it will not significantly decrease the bear population and at the same time reduce the total amount of horrific deaths that bears often suffer.

5

Predacious Encounters and Attacks

Predatory *attacks* are easy to classify because of the bear's obvious attempt to, or success at, eating the person. Predatory *encounters,* where the person escapes or kills the bear, are not easy to confirm. I interpret the following three accounts as predatory encounters, and the last two are clearly predatory attacks.

Lee Foster is the silvicultural planner for the Ministry of Forests at Vanderhoof, B.C. Lee is very interested in bear hazard safety and has provided information on the subject to Ministry of Forests employees. In the following encounter Lee had to make some quick decisions:

Dear Gary:
As per your request here is a brief account of my black bear encounter that happened on June 13, 1988 at approximately mile 73 on the Alaska Highway.

It was another warm, breezy spring day in the Peace River area. Working as a Resource Assistant with the Ministry of Forests, I was out inspecting a block that had been sheared and piled the previous winter with the intentions of determining a second pass treatment. The access was poor, so I walked the last 400 metres into the block. Enroute, mid-sized bear tracks were evident on the relatively dry road surface.

With the possible presence of a bear in the vicinity and no protection in any form, I made a mental note of staying out in the open. As I approached the far end of the opening, I remembered a natural spring which I had noted the previous winter, just off the edge of the block. I entered the stand of trees and approached the spring which was approximately 75 metres from the clearing. I was in the process of taking a drink from the spring when a sixth sense told me that something wasn't quite right. I quickly moved away from the site and at about 40 metres I heard a branch snap behind me.

I turned around and spotted a mid-sized black bear where I had previously been only seconds before. I have had a few encounters with bears and had never seen any that wouldn't run when confronted. My first impulse was to yell at him, fully expecting him to turn and run.

If I had thought a little more about this I would have just slipped quietly and quickly out of there. The bear already had wind of me and knew I was somewhere in the vicinity, yet had not actually pinpointed me.

However, as I yelled he did the opposite of what I anticipated and ran directly at me, covering the 40 metres at an incredible rate. I stood my ground and at approximately eight metres distance he came to a stop and stood up on his hind legs.

Needless to say, my adrenaline glands were working overtime and the bear, although not making any noise, made it quite apparent by his expression that he had more than curiosity on his mind.

Standing there without so much as a pocket knife I felt rather naked and turned to grab a large stick which lay right behind me. No sooner had I commenced my move than the bear was on all fours lunging at me. I quickly regained my defensive position with the stick raised over my head. This caused the bear to halt his charge and he once more stood up, this time within striking range of me.

I stood a foot taller than the bear and I would estimate his size at approximately five feet and 250 pounds. I am not embarrassed to say that those few seconds that I stood face-to-face with that bear were the most terrifying of my life, knowing full well what his intentions were, and fully expecting him to carry them out. However, much to my relief, he seemed to suddenly lose his nerve and he wheeled around and left as quickly as he approached. Needless to say, I didn't waste any time heading back to my vehicle.

As a parting comment, I would like to emphasize that encounters like this are not frequent, however they are common enough that if you spend a lot of time in the woods your chances are relatively good that you could have an encounter of a similar nature. Depending on your personality and that of the bear the end result may not be quite as successful. Needless to say, this event definitely emphasized the need to put up with the inconvenience of packing a firearm for protection from bears as well as the necessity of providing adequate training to all field staff on bear behaviour and defense measures.

Lee Foster, R.P.F., Silviculture Planner
Vanderhoof Forest District

* * *

Scott Whittemore is an avid backpacker who has recently published a book entitled *The Bella Coola Valley And Vicinity Hiking Trails And Routes* (1993). The following story is an encounter he had in the Rainbow Mountains of South Tweedsmuir Park just Northeast of Bella Coola, and is taken from his journal:

. . .

The next morning was spectacular. I awoke at 7:00 a.m. to the sound of caribou racing by my tent. The sun had not yet risen on the horizon, but the sky was pink and reminded me of the night before. The hills close behind me glowed like Ayres Rock in Australia and the location of quartz crystals was revealed by the low lying sun.

I soaked in the beauty of the morning, washed up, prayed, and ate breakfast. I laid around waiting for the dew to dry from my tent before I would pack it up. At 10:20, I was ready to continue my trip.

I headed west from Crystal Lake, descending down a narrow pass, but by a stream that was almost dried up. To the left is "Ayres Rock", or at least that is what it seemed to me.

. . .

This was my third time in this pass, and I have never felt comfortable in it. Perhaps because it is difficult to leave behind the open alpine country and get used to the enclosed dark forest environment. It's difficult to adjust from a countryside where one can see for five or ten kilometres, across rolling hills and down shallow valleys, to a forest where a tree only three feet away can hide much from the hiker's view.

I never packed a gun on this trip because I did
not think I would need it. I figured that all the
bears would be fishing on the Dean or Bella
Coola Rivers, far below where I was. I never
dreamed of a bear encounter, except in a dusty
part of my mind that is willing to accept any
possibilities.

The patches of scrubby trees started to give way
to a thick forest or alpine fir. The view was
squelched to nil and sunlight was competing
with darkness.

I passed a twisted tree at a point where the forest seemed particularly dark. The surrounding ingredients almost spooked me and triggered a debate within my mind. One part of
my thoughts was telling me to make some
vocal noises, just in case a bear was around.
Another thought was saying that it was a ridiculous idea - there are no bears around. Finally
I agreed with the point that said "it won't hurt to
make a few shouts", and so I did.

Within a minute or two of my shouts, I heard
some crackling of dry branches. It obviously
wasn't the scratchy sound of a squirrel clinging to a tree, or jumping onto a branch. No, the
sounds were of a lower tone, something
imposed by large game. My mind went
through a checklist of animals that it could be:
Possibly deer, but I had never before seen signs
of them in this area; maybe the caribou I had
seen the night before, but what would they be
doing in such a thick tangled forest; a bear? -
no they are fishing; I know, it could be a moose.
Well?!

I shouted more, and the breaking of branches
continued. There were at least two animals in
the bush. I was on a switchback part of the trail.
One animal was above me and a second was
almost parallel to the trail I was on; it was off

the end of the trail, but I couldn't tell if it was 50, 100, or 200 feet away from me. The crackling continued, but not in a hurried pace. I decided to attempt to determine just what was in the bush, so I would at least know what to expect from the creature. I stayed on the trail and started to get a glimpse of the creature moving up the hill, from beyond the direction I was heading. The other creature that created the noise above me was definitely too far to be seen. At last I saw the rear of a bear. It looked black, with a thick coat of fur and an obvious tail. I was glad that it was heading uphill, and I down. (It looked as if the bear had departed the trail when I had first yelled and headed straight up the hill-side.)

I pulled out my buck knife as I continued downhill. I knew it wasn't much for protection, but it was all that I had. I noticed my heart pounding fast and loudly. After nearly five minutes of walking, I relaxed more and put away the knife. I figured there was enough distance between me and those bears, but I continued to give out shouts to oust the bears up. I continued to hike for at least a few minutes more, possibly five.

The nightmare was about to begin.

It took a few moments for my mind to make sense of the sound of rapid footprints coming down the switchback that I had just left. I had never heard such a sound before. It was the sound of a horse's hoofs hitting the ground when in a full gallop. But the footsteps were softer sounding and the pace more rapid. Fear shot through me and I thought "oh shit"!

"When I turned to look behind me, a bear stood at a full stop, barely 30 feet away. Its head was hanging somewhat and I could see the color of its eyes - golden brown. Its fur was

dark brown, almost black and its snout was a
tan color. There was no hump on its back, so I
figured that it must be a black bear rather than
a grizzly.

I just stood there looking at the bear. I figured
that it now had had a good sniff and look at me
and would be on its own way! Instead it lowered its head further, opened its mouth, stuck
out its tongue, and then made a barely audible
crying noise. Again its mouth opened and a
tongue momentarily hung out. Its head was
still low. To my shock it stepped forward.

I remembered Stanley Edwards telling a story
of a bear that pushed its way into his 8' x 10'
home. He described it having soft, gentle
brown eyes. I searched this bear's eyes for gen-
tleness, but could only see a hard and determined look (and possibly some fear). It stepped
forward again, slowly, very slowly, but without
a break in its forward motion from the last
step. It continued toward me with a slow but
steady pace.

My mind was recalling masses of information that I had collected over the years for a time
like this. An encounter that I always feared,
but now there was no room for fear. I spoke to
the bear softly and then more loudly; a yell
seemed unnecessary and possibly a catalyst to
a faster attack upon me. The bear continued
forward without hesitation from its pursuit.

By this time I had unclipped my backpack
waist belt and had carefully taken a step or two
backwards. I kept being reminded not to make
any sudden moves, but as careful as I was, it
seemed that I just couldn't be smooth enough. I
slid the pack down my back, onto my buttocks,
and finally down my left leg to the ground. I
leaned it against a small log that was next to
me. I had never imagined that I would leave

behind my backpack for a bear.

The bear continued to creep forward and I backwards, or more like sideways, away from the bear. I glanced to my right and checked out two trees for climbing, but I decided they were too far and the bear was too close; besides, I figured that it would just climb them anyway.

By this time the bear had reached my pack and I was feeling very hopeful. We were probably no more than 20 feet apart. The bear slowly moved his nose to the sweaty pack off my back and sniffed it for a second or two. To my horror he continued to move forward, past the pack, towards me.

There was little left for me to do. I strongly heard the warnings that a person should never run from a bear. However, I wasn't ready to lie down and play dead, and the bear was moving closer. My options were minimal. I increased my pace away from the bear and immediately increased my distance between he and I. However, his pace also quickened. He was still in pursuit of me. I ran harder, continually looking over my shoulder to monitor the situation. Every time the bear and I went into a dip in the trail (and the bear's head was not visible), I would accelerate my speed. I was gaining ground. What a relief!

For about 250-300 feet the bear chased after me. At one time I looked back and it was nearly at a halt. I slowed down and then stopped, when I noticed that it had halted its pursuit. It was about 75 feet away from me, with its side to me, but still watching my actions. It was remarkable; the bear had let me get away!!

I watched the bear for something near a minute long. He held his ground; for a moment I thought that if he retreated, I could return for my gear. Then I decided that I had been exceptionally lucky to still be alive and that I would not push my chances. I headed to the Rainbow cabin, 1 km away. Many times I turned around to see if that bear had decided to continue its pursuit.

. . .

As calculated, I was at the road by 5:30 p.m. Karl Harestad picked me up. He was heading towards Anahim Lake, but when we passed an on-coming vehicle, he made a u-turn and caught up to the car. It was Diane Tuck and she apprehensively provided me with a ride to the Valley.

(By this time I was quite tired). I had last eaten at 7:30-8:00 a.m. and hiked 37 km."

Author's note: Scott called me the night he got back and told me his story. He asked me if I thought it was worth going back for his pack and the camera gear in it. I explained to him that by the description of the bear's behaviour, it was not a habituated bear, and because his food was in sealed containers, his gear may be okay. Two days later, when Scott got back to his pack, accompanied by an armed friend, he was surprised to find his pack untouched.

Setting the pack down to distract the bear was a good idea, but this will not work with all bears. The first few minutes of this encounter were critical; Scott kept facing the bear, and the bear never quite got the confidence to press the attack. This bear had probably never seen a human before, and may have previously killed small mammals. Scott was very lucky.

* * *

In the following letter, addressed to the R.C.M.P., you will discern the frustration that many Canadians feel about the federal government's determination to make it difficult for honest, law-abiding citizens to obtain and use firearms for sporting activities or defense. There are many types of outdoor work where carrying a rifle or shotgun is very difficult. Handguns clearly have a legitimate place under these circumstances:

NCO i/c RCMPolice
Firearms Section
657 West 37th Avenue
Vancouver, B.C.

Dear Sir/Madam:

I have noticed an increase in the paperwork to apply for a permit to carry a firearm. While the intent to restrict undesirable people access to these weapons is good, I hope your department still realizes that these tools are essential to ensure safety of workers in remote areas that are populated by predatory animals.

I would like to share an experience that recently happened to me while working in the woods just 60 km west of Prince George. On July 5, 1993, summer student Al Baxter and I were hanging pheromones (chemical beetle attractents) in a timber stand not 500 m from our pickup. This work would take about one hour. I did not bring my gun for such a short time in the woods due to concerns of what to do with the gun for the remainder of the work day.

About 1:00 p.m. while walking 50 m parallel to my partner, I heard a grunt and snort to my right. I immediately started to walk away from the sound. Then the noise became apparent as the bear came charging toward me. I ran approximately 15 feet to a limby pine tree yelling and climbing as fast as possible. The bear lunged at the tree on the opposite side and started climbing up after me. She was catching up to me, snarling and snapping. I had a good hold on the branches and with an attempt to fight off the bear, I kicked her as hard as I could in the nose. The bear slid down the tree and began to circle wildly and tear up the ground.

My partner, Al, was running toward me, thinking I was being mauled. The bear, hearing him, charged toward Al's location. I yelled to Al to climb a tree and he did. The bear then climbed the tree Al was in, in an attempt to wrestle him to the ground. Al threw his hardhat at her face and struck the young black bear with a stick he had brought up the tree with him. The bear retreated to the ground and continued to charge between Al and me (about 50 m apart) for 15 to 20 minutes.

Over the next four hours the bear circled us, sometimes disappearing for 15 minutes and then reappearing, snorting and grinding her teeth. Finally around 5:00 p.m. the bear climbed a large Douglas-fir tree about 30 m away from my location, I presume to get a closer look at us. She stayed up the tree for the next 15 minutes. We decided Al would try to climb down while I watched and talked to the bear distracting her. Al had a 15 minute walk back to the pickup to radio for help.

Another 40 minutes went by until help arrived with a rifle.

The bear for some reason remained in the tree. The bear was shot and I climbed out of the pine tree around 6:15 p.m.

The next morning we reported the incident to Fish and Wildlife who determined from the events that the bear was most probably hunting us for food. This occurrence is an excellent example when a revolver would have been very, very effective. I consider us very lucky to have not been seriously injured or worse.

I thought my writing to you and communicating this near-miss event would emphasize the need for firearm protection in jobs such as ours; a fact that should be taken very seriously.

Yours truly,

CANADIAN FOREST PRODUCTS
Isle Pierre Division
Duncan McKellar, RPF
Forestry Supervisor
Al Baxter
Summer Student

Author's note: There are several interesting elements in this story. The bear was no doubt looking for a meal, but showed considerable anger throughout the incident, then became tree-climbing defensive at the end. Al was very smart to have taken a limb with him up the tree; this may have saved his life. In many attacks like this one, the black bear latched on to the person's foot and dragged them from the tree for the kill.

* * *

The following bear attack story was supplied by *The Kamloops Daily News*:

Man beats off bear to save his friend
By Susan Duncan
Daily News City Editor

A forestry worker who beat a black bear off his partner Tuesday, and then helped the wounded man run a kilometre to safety, downplayed his heroism today.

"At first, I didn't know what to do. It flashed

through my mind to run," Pritchard resident
Stan Thiessen said. "I wondered, 'If I hit the
bear, now is it my turn?'"

He took the risk, picked up a stick and started
beating on the bear that had timber cruiser
Robin Proppe, 24, pinned to the ground by the
neck.

"I don't know, I just grabbed a stick and
started whaling on it. It turned around and
looked right at me."

The terrifying incident began in the woods
about 1:00 p.m. near North Barriere Lake.

Proppe, a Barriere resident, and Thiessen
were staking out an area for logging when
Thiessen spotted a bear below him. He said he
began making noise so the bear would know
they were in the area.

For unexplained reasons, the bear must have
circled around the men and suddenly attacked
Proppe.

"He definitely stalked us," said Thiessen, a
seasoned outdoors man.

He said he only realized it had attacked when
Proppe came running past him with the bear
close behind.

The bear, believed to be a male, had just
charged Proppe and knocked him over.

Proppe climbed a small tree, but the bear
pulled him down by the leg and bit into his
neck.

"Robin was screaming 'Stan, help me, help
me.'"

Forestry consultant Mike Pagdin, who
employed Proppe and Thiessen, said today that
Proppe told him he could hear a grinding sound
when the bear was on him.

"He's got some nasty cuts on the back of his
neck about 3 1/2 inches long and 1 1/2 inches
deep. It crunched the bone in the back of his

neck, but there was no bone damage," Pagdin said after visiting Proppe at Royal Inland Hospital.

"He's still pretty shook up. It was a terrifying experience. He wouldn't have survived if Stan hadn't been there," Pagdin said.

After Thiessen got the bear off, he pulled Proppe to his feet and told him not to run, just to stay together. Both had sticks and were beating at the bear as they walked quickly toward their truck, said Thiessen.

"He just kept coming at us, he kept coming. There were numerous times we'd stop and fight that bear with sticks or rocks or anything we could get our hands on."

He said the bear followed them for 30-45 minutes and was often only three metres away. Eventually they reached a clearing and the bear dropped back about 15 metres, and they realized they would be able to make it to the truck.

Thiessen said he had a rifle in the truck and would have gone after the bear immediately, but knew he had to get Proppe to the hospital.

Both Thiessen and Pagdin said they don't want the story to come across as though bears are a menace.

"The bears are doing their thing," Pagdin said. "That's their bush. We're working in their area."

Thiessen said he'll go back in the bush, but "I'm packing a 12-gauge now."

Author's note: It is important to understand the level of aggression that this bear displayed. These two men had to fight the bear right back to the truck. It is extremely doubtful that one person could have "fought back" and survived this attack. Robin and Stan told me that they now carry pepper spray or shotguns while working in the field.

* * *

Jim Hart is the District Conservation Officer in Fort Nelson, B.C. He has been gathering bear attack information from the Northeast part of the province since the middle 1980s. This information has been sent to Stephen Herrero for his research.

Jim has had great difficulty trying to convince anyone South of the 57th parallel, except Herrero and myself, that there is a significant predacious black bear problem in his part of the world.

Jim is one of those special people who takes death prevention seriously. I believe that through his efforts to educate people about predacious behaviour, and to let them know that it is all right to kill bears exhibiting that behaviour, he has saved at least three or four lives in the last eight years.

When I started this book, I decided that I would not include many human death stories as I didn't want the sensational aspect of these types of stories to influence the technical nature of this book. However, I am including the following story from Jim Hart's file to provide a clear picture of the possible outcome of a predatory encounter.

Statement of Jabez Kruithof of Hornby Island, B.C., taken May 30, 1985 @ 10:15 hrs:

Statement taken in presence of Conservation Officer Jim Hart.

I met Gordy Ray here in town about 12:00 noon on the 29th of May. We had lunch together then decided to go explore whether or not he could make it with his machine, as he is in seedling delivery. So we went to base camp and left at roughly 2:45 p.m. with two trikes

and went up to the Tackama old road south of
the radio tower. We surveyed access to the
river and spotted our first bear there at the old
well site. Then we parked the trikes and went
through the first cut-block south. Getting into
the second cut-block we spotted another bear.
We waited till he was up into the other cut-
block. He never spotted us. We went further
south for another 20 minute walk, then we
turned around. We got to that little stretch of
forest where the incident occurred. I heard the
bear, heard something crashing through the
woods, turned around and saw the bear roughly
12 feet away. We backed off slowly toward the
other side of the road facing the bear. Then
Gordy broke into a run into the woods and I
climbed the first available little tree along the
road. Gordy climbed a small tree roughly ten
feet behind me, and we started to throw sticks at
the bear, shouting and screaming to see if he
would take off. However the bear did not take
off, he circled the tree I was in, then moved
away roughly 12 feet. I had told the bear to
"screw off". I turned around and said to Gordy
I think he understands this language. Gordy
then began yelling the same thing. Gordy said
he was having a hard time holding on. I
shouted at him to hold on. Gordy fell, and the
bear went for him from roughly 25 feet away.
Gordy ran away, made about ten feet, and the
bear caught up to him. I shouted at Gordy to
stand still, but I don't think he heard me.
Gordy took a stick and hit the bear on the face
for roughly five or ten seconds. The bear took
him, walked right over him and covered him.
The bear's head was right level with Gordy's
head. The bear was lengthwise. I shouted at
Gordy to roll up in a ball but, again, I don't
think he heard me. Gordy was screaming and

the bear barely moved off him and began rolling Gordy around. That's when I saw the first
blood - it looked like it was from his hands. I
felt helpless and climbed down the tree wanting to do something; I realized I could do nothing and climbed back up. I heard Gordy yell
"Help." I realized I could not do anything to
help him. I climbed down the tree as quietly as
possible, walked away, and then feeling safe I
started running. This incident occurred about
5:40 in the afternoon. It took me roughly one-
and-a-quarter hours to get back to where the trikes were parked. I started up the trike, drove
away and another black bear came towards
me, roughly 300-400 feet away. I drove full
speed towards it and it took off into the woods.
Then I went up the old road to the old Alaska
Highway to get back to camp. At the first wash-
out coming from the north, I met Trevor
Grimshaw packing up the helicopter. I asked
him if he had a mobile and if he would get me a
helicopter, as a person had been mauled by a
bear. This was roughly 8:10 p.m. I asked Trevor to pack a gun. I heard him ask for a gun
over the radio. Then I waited till sometime
around 8:30 when the other chopper arrived
with the paramedic. Trevor's helicopter was
loaded on the back of a truck because of a
mechanical breakdown. We then flew and
landed approximately 800 feet away from the
place of the incident. Trevor and I went looking for Gordon. Coming to the place of the incident, I spotted Gordon's jacket 50-60 feet in the
bush. That's the moment the bear came lunging down a small creek at full speed towards
us, from the right side of the road. Trevor
kneeled down and shot the bear when it was
about six to eight feet away from him. The bear
turned, ran for ten feet and Trevor shot him for

the second time. I had turned away when I saw the bear come at us and I stood by the nearest tree. After the shooting I went to the chopper to get the paramedic and Trevor went to Gordon's body. When I came back with the paramedic, Trevor said that he had just spotted another bear but could not get a good aim at it. The paramedic checked out Gordon's body and said he was dead. We hung around for a little while then Trevor went to the helicopter and I believe he sent the helicopter to get the R.C.M.P. We waited for 45-50 minutes and then the chopper came back with you people (Conservation Officers).

Author's note: There has been considerable resistance by many people to accept that predatory behavior exists in black bears because this would mean that bears can have intrinsic aggression towards people. We can no longer consider predacious black bear behaviour "rare"; this is a foolish and dangerous idea.

6

Bear Avoidance

The first line of defense against bears is avoidance. There are two types of avoidance: initial planning and site-specific. In my bear hazard safety courses for government ministries, I suggest that these ministries create a district bear hazard map. Bear encounters can happen anywhere, but bear high-use areas must be identified when planning field work or recreation. This information can be obtained from Fisheries, Parks, Forestry, Fish and Wildlife, Conservation Officers, biologists, guides, trappers, etc. Exact locations and time of year are important. In the *Bear Biology* chapter, I briefly outlined the types of habitat that bears use at different times of the year, but it is important to gather information specific to your area. Avoid bear high-use areas if possible.

In areas of high bear hazard with reasonably open terrain, field personnel should do helicopter fly-overs to assess numbers and locations of bears.

Whenever possible, field workers should work in pairs - this substantially increases the ability to survive a bear attack, or any kind of incident.

Site-specific avoidance means learning to recognize bear sign and high-use areas, understanding bear aggressive behaviour, and employing certain techniques to make bears aware of your presence.

The bear signs that you should be looking for are the

following: beds, tracks, diggings, over-turned
rocks, ripped-apart logs, droppings, and rub trees. If
you take time to observe and learn bear sign, you
will eventually be able to assess how much bear
activity there is in an area.

Sow grizzly and first-year cub tracks.   *Gary Shelton*

If you are a forestry engineer putting in a cut-block
line along the edge of a mid-elevation slide area in
May or June, and you see two or three fresh bear beds,
that's telling you something. If you are walking
along an old logging road in August and you step
over three or four piles of bear droppings loaded with

berry seeds in a distance of a kilometre or two, that's telling you something. If you are hiking along a river in October and you see fresh scrape marks on a tree, some digging in a dry channel, and part of a salmon laying on the bank ahead, that's telling you something.

Large male grizzly track.   *Gary Shelton*

In all of these circumstances a person should back off, or if that's not possible, slow down, do lots of look-ing, and make plenty of noise. In semi-open or alpine areas a person can use binoculars to carefully look over a planned travel route.

Bear sensory capability is different from that of most other animals. Their eyesight is about the same as ours, but with some serious deficiencies. If bears see color it must be poorly; they do not have good peripheral vision or depth perception beyond a short distance. They cannot define stationary objects beyond about 100 metres. These are general statements, as some aspects of sight recognition capability are learned; I have seen a few individual bears with capabilities beyond what I have indicated, and some with less. Bears in parks that have repeated exposure to people probably learn to recognize them quickly and at longer distances.

Their hearing is four or five times better than ours, but far short of deer, moose, goats, etc. Their primary sense is the sense of smell, which is exceptional, but of course is limited to up-wind. If you were walking over the crest of a sharp ridge with a stiff wind blowing in your face, and a bear was bedded just over the top, you would be on it before either you or the bear knew it. If you were any other animal than human, you would have smelled the bear long before. Mostly we have our sight; mainly what bears have is their up-wind smell. In many cases, this is a deadly combination.

Humans must avoid close-range surprise encounters. The way in which a bear reacts at ten metres, versus 100 metres, is significantly different. Keeping track of the wind is important; keep a lighter in your front pocket for this purpose. The best way to let bears know you are coming is the use of sound. Many people have small bells attached to their packs for this purpose. This system is usually adequate, but not with high wind or around river noise. The bear that was bedded just over the hill in stiff wind conditions, for example, probably wouldn't have heard the high-pitched bell soon enough.

That bear would, however, have heard a very loud yell, or a toot from an hand-held boat horn - one toot halfway up the hill, and another just before the top. Two toots are necessary because most animals wait for a second sensory input before fleeing. Most bears will identify a yell or an airhorn sound with people and leave, but not all will. A bear with no human experience, or a habituated bear, may not flee from human sounds. A predacious bear may actually be attracted by sounds. Medium-pitched bells and airhorns in noisy or thick vegetation situations, combined with human voices, is the best we can do.

Snow-slide country is bear country.   *Gary Shelton*

Forestry engineers must be particularly careful while working near avalanche chutes and slide

areas during spring and early summer. Snow disturbance areas usually have excellent bear feed and
bears like to bed down in the timber next to these
openings.   Quite often there is creek noise near
where they are bedded, and if you are travelling into
the wind, you can walk right up on a bear.

Burns have tremendous forage in them for bears and other
wildlife.   *Gary Shelton*

I hear many stories from people who work in the
field who have had bear encounters in burns and logging slashes. This type of habitat is often loaded with
berries and other excellent bear food, especially if

there is a slow deciduous regeneration cycle going on. These areas often present additional hazards because the bush can be thick.

Any time you are in the field and get the smell of rotten meat, or walk up on what appears to be a kill disturbance on the ground, back up quickly and quietly at least 200 metres and carefully assess the situation.

These kill disturbances are usually from six to 12 metres in diameter and will look like something has raked ground litter and soil into a pile. Sometimes the carcass is buried in pieces and a large pile is not evident, or the bear is just about finished with the carcass and the pile is spread around.

There are usually plenty of birds around a carcass, and plenty of bird noise. If you hear lots of raven and other bird noise from a fixed spot for over ten or 15 minutes, be suspicious of a carcass.

Make sure you are not approaching a carcass with a bear nearby. If possible leave the area. If you must proceed, make at least a 200 metre detour around the area.

Any time hunters return to animals that they have previously killed, they should be armed and should start making loud yells from 200 metres distance. Approach slowly and watch for bear sign. In some areas bears have learned to respond to gunshots, and may try to take a kill from a hunter. Do not argue with a grizzly over a carcass; you may end up losing the battle.

There has been considerable speculation on whether women should go into bear country while menstruating. I have found no direct evidence that this is a danger, but I have heard many stories of bears following women in this situation, and there may be something to it.

I've never worried about wearing after-shave lotion around bears; however, when I used to guide, some hunters would ask if I wasn't afraid the smoke from my cigar might scare off game. I always told them that if an animal can smell my cigar, it can smell me. Besides, the cigar was for wind testing to ensure that we were always down-wind or cross-wind from an animal we were stalking.

Most bears would be attracted to any blood or food smell; bears who are afraid of people would be repelled by a human smell; habituated park bears, or wild predatory bears, would probably be attracted by any smell. And it may be possible that bears can smell humans at longer distances if humans are wearing a lotion or perfume; this could possibly attract the wrong kind of bear.

Grizzlies have evolved an open-habitat defensive behaviour and they have a charge-then-retreat relationship with wolves. Thousands of times in the past, grizzlies and wolves have contested the possession of a carcass. Grizzlies usually get their way by chasing wolves off. Because of this, it is generally not a good idea to take dogs into grizzly country. Dogs *are* wolves to unhabituated grizzly bears, and they may chase your dog back to you. A case in point: On a September evening in 1983, our dog was raising a fuss behind the barn. We went out to see if it was the same bear that my daughter Julie had earlier encountered while riding her horse. As we approached the creek, the dog jumped into the water and stood barking about four metres from a grizzly who was eating a fish. Julie and my son Tyler were right behind me and when I saw the potential of the situation, I told them to back up quickly. The bear went for the dog, almost catching her, and didn't stop chasing her until it reached us - had we still been standing there.

I also had a six-month-old German Shepherd ruined by a grizzly - the bear chased the dog right up to and under the house. After that he would always head for the crawl space when he smelled any kind of bear.

On the other hand, I know of some cases where dogs have saved people from grizzlies, and some races of dogs, or properly trained ones, can hold a grizzly without bringing it back to their owners. A dog on a leash is an excellent warning device, but don't let it get loose unless it is properly trained.

Most black bears will run from dogs, but not all. I have heard some stories of black bears chasing dogs back to their owners.

I have heard two stories where people whistled at grizzlies in alpine to get their attention, and were shocked to see the bear run toward them. Grizzlies are highly attuned to marmot whistles, so avoid whistling in alpine where there are grizzlies.

BEAR AVOIDANCE SUMMARY:

1. Obtain bear high-use area information when planning field work or recreation.
2. Do helicopter fly-overs in high-use work areas before commencing work.
3. Work in pairs whenever possible.
4. Take time to become familiar with bear sign. You will eventually be able to assess the amount of recent bear activity.
5. Attach a medium-pitch bell to your pack, but use loud yells or a boat horn when circumstances require it.
6. When in open or semi-open country, look over planned routes with binoculars.
7. Forestry engineers must be careful around slides and avalanche chutes in spring and early summer.
8. Always expect to encounter bears in burns and logging slashes.
9. Slow down and make plenty of noise when in or near berry patches.
10. Any time you smell rotten meat or see evidence of a bear kill, quickly and quietly go

back the way you came, at least 200 metres.
Pay attention to bird noise. Leave the area if
possible, or circle around at least 200 metres.
11. Hunters must be careful when returning to
a kill.
12. Menstruating women may choose to avoid
bear hazard exposure.
13. Do not take dogs into grizzly country
unless on a leash.
14. Avoid having any food, blood smells, or
cosmetics with you if possible.
15. Do not whistle in alpine grizzly country.

One last point about bear avoidance: Everyone must
share the responsibility of not teaching bears to associate food or garbage with people. Do not leave lunch
sacks or food scraps anywhere that bears can find
them. If a young bear finds food in conjunction with
human smell several times, it will become a bear
that you cannot avoid.
No matter how good people become at avoiding
bears, there will still be bear encounters; that is the
subject of the next chapter.

7

Bear Encounters

My definition for a bear encounter is related to bear behaviour: Any time a bear becomes aware of you and must make the decision of fight-or-flight, you have had an encounter. Habituated bears, and sometimes young curious bears, do not possess this behaviour in relation to humans. Fight-or-flight behaviour is based on perceived threat, but bears run into other animals all the time and they can't always run away, or they wouldn't get any eating done. Thus bears must quickly decide whether the intruder is dangerous, neutral, or potential food. Sometimes it takes a little while to decide, unless the animal is close.

GRIZZLY ENCOUNTERS

In about half of the grizzly encounters I've had on the B.C. Coast, the bear made at least a minor overt threat before leaving. Single grizzlies usually depart quickly, but will sometimes blow, growl, pop their teeth, swat the ground or a tree, or make a short bluff charge. Sows with cubs are a different matter, especially if you're within about 75 metres. Most of the sow-grizzly-with-cubs encounters I've had were similar to my following experience:

In September of 1973, I was hunting deer along

the Bella Coola River. As I was walking slowly through a brushy area into the wind, a grizzly stood up from a bed about 50 metres to my left, immediately made a short, fast blow sound, and stood up on its hind legs. Then two first-year cubs stood up, looking around and whining. I put a round into the chamber, pushed the safety off, and stood absolutely still. The sow dropped to all fours with ears back and spinal hair on end, then made two lunges towards me, flinging her front legs outward between jumps. With each lunge she made an in-and-out, half blow-half growl sound. She spun around and hit the ground in front of the cubs, sending debris flying into the air; the cubs both bawled and started running away in the opposite direction. The sow turned back towards me, this time at a 45 degree angle, then went stiff-legged and bounced sideways towards me, blowing with each bounce. She turned and ran back about ten metres, stopped, spun around, and stood up on her hind legs. She then put her nose straight up, searching the air for my scent. She growled as she dropped down and came forward again in a lunging frontal charge with terrifying in-and-out blow/growl sounds; she came to a skidding halt only ten metres away from me, holding her head sideways with her mouth open and froth dripping to the ground. I had the gun sighted; she was at the boundary line of having time for only one shot; she lifted her head, spun around, and was out of sight in seconds.

At this point I don't have to tell you that the most important piece of spare equipment to carry in bear country is extra under-shorts.

Most encounters with grizzly bears go the way we want - the bear departs without making contact. But in two of the sow grizzly encounters I've had, I barely got the killing shot off before they got their paws on me.

DANGEROUS GRIZZLY ENCOUNTERS

There are four types of encounters with grizzly bears that are extremely dangerous. The first three types involve sows with cubs, and are variations on their typical defensive-aggressive response:

1. **When first-year cubs go up a tree**: This doesn't happen often, but when it does, the sow will usually make contact quickly with any perceived threat within about 75 metres, and sometimes much further.

In the fall of 1977, I walked up on a sow with two first-year cubs that were bedded down by two small fir trees. I had crossed the river below them, walked upstream along the bottom of a steep three-metre bank, crawled up the bank and then stood up. I heard a low growl to my left, and there they were. When the sow started displaying her annoyance with me, the two cubs each stood up against the two fir trees and hooked their claws in the bark. I don't believe they would have gone up the trees if the sow hadn't run around the trees, then stood up in a three-quarter leaning-forward stance and growled.

When she growled, the two cubs lunged up the trees. The sow took a short look at them and instantly a behavioural response was triggered. I was no more than 20 metres from her, and unfortunately I had to kill her. She had made two lunges before I touched the trigger.

2. **When second-year cubs join in on bluff charges:** It is my opinion that occasionally some sow grizzlies with second-year cubs

develop a family defense behaviour. In the middle of their second year the cubs stop running away when a threat is nearby, and start joining their mother in threat displaying against the intruder. This behaviour would have tremendous survival value as the family group would be able to defend and stay with food sources during the most critical period for keeping the group well-fed.

In the last 29 years we have had four grizzly families develop this behaviour in the Bella Coola Valley, and I have heard or read of six other accounts. Encountering a family group with this behaviour can be very dangerous, especially if circumstances are such that you cannot quickly increase your distance from the cubs.

3. When a sow with cubs charges from a long distance in open ground without bluffing: I haven't a clue what this behaviour is about, but the first sow that almost got me behaved this way.

I learned something very important when this sow was charging down a steep hill-side towards me - something I teach in my firearms defense course: When a bear is coming full-tilt in a frontal running charge, the body is moving up and down and the head is changing position in relation to the body. It's therefore impossible to pick a spot to shoot above or below the head. In this circumstance, shoot dead center of the body mass, or you will likely miss the vital area.

It took all the determination and strength I had to force myself to pull off a good shot against that sow. There was time for just one shot, and I had to jump sideways or she would have rolled over on top of me.

4. When a grizzly is defending a carcass:

Everybody has heard of this one, and it's every bit true. Grizzly bears have evolved an extremely aggressive carcass defense behaviour that has caused many human deaths.

I learned a lot about this behaviour in grizzlies during the first ten years I lived in the Bella Coola Valley. I would take problem black bear carcasses that I had killed and place them far out in the bush where no one would ever go, then return every few days to see what was going on.

I was lucky to have survived this study (I killed some grizzlies as a result of it), but I learned much about the dissection, burying, and come-and-go carcass feeding behaviour of grizzlies.

OTHER GRIZZLY ENCOUNTERS

Predatory attacks by grizzly bears are not common, but I believe they will become more common as we inflict less mortality on bold bears; a person will have to do *everything* right to survive this type of encounter. I have heard several accounts of sow grizzlies with second-year cubs stalking people predaciously in the spring, when bears are hunting moose or caribou calves. Bears hunt by smell, and if very hungry, become frenzied as they get closer to the target.

On several occasions I have had grizzlies act aggressively towards me because they mistook me for another bear. In the latter part of October 1985, I spent a day grizzly hunting in an area down-river from my place that could only be accessed with a drift boat. I had hunted into the wind for about two hours and was ready to head back to the boat. I quietly waded across a thigh-deep slough; on the other side, I carefully crawled to the top of a steep bank, and just as I was standing up, I heard a deep growl about 15 metres from me behind a wall of thick brush. I put a shell in the chamber, slipped the safety off, and stood absolutely still. I didn't want the bear to zero in on exactly where I was.

I knew it had heard, but not smelled me. The bear started huffing and growling, and I started getting nervous, because I was too close. I couldn't see the bear, but all of a sudden I saw the top of a small sapling bend over and disappear behind the brush. I could hear the bear walking back and forth and growling; twice more I saw the top of a sapling bend down out of sight.

This encounter went on for four or five minutes; then dead silence. I waited another five minutes, then slowly moved along the top of the bank away from the bear. It was the longest encounter I had ever had, and I felt thoroughly intimidated, almost scared. I walked away with my shoulders a couple of notches lower.

The next day I went back with a friend, Randy Svisdahl, and we were able to determine that I had walked up on a very large male who was bedded down and defending his favorite fishing hole against other bears.

A few months later I watched a film about bears that Tommy Thompkins had made. In one segment of the film he had caught two male grizzlies making threat displays towards each other. One of the bears would repeatedly straddle small saplings or brush and push them over. This is what the bear I had encountered was doing in an attempt to intimidate what he thought was another bear.

I categorize attacks in relation to the type of behaviour involved, but any surprise close-range encounter with a grizzly has potential to be deadly. At close range a grizzly feels severely threatened and the intensity of the aggression is substantially increased, no matter what the particular type of behavioural motivation is.

BLACK BEAR ENCOUNTERS

Black bear encounters usually take some different twists. Black bears have a defensive-aggressive behaviour similar to grizzlies, but with much less chance of contact. In the initial stage of an encounter where they have chosen to stand their ground, black bears will quite often do bluffing displays, including false charges to warn the threat to retreat. But they will usually run away quite quickly, or run a short distance then climb a tree.

Black bear sows with cubs can be more dangerous if you're too close. If you are 50 metres or more away, they will usually send the cubs up a tree, stand at the base, and blow, pop their teeth, and growl. If you are closer they may follow through with a charge to make sure you understand the message. If a sow just had a major battle with a boar that tried to kill her cubs, she may come all the way and do you serious damage. Since it is impossible to know what may have just gone on before your encounter, all bears should be treated with the same degree of caution.

The most important behaviour to watch for in black bears is predatory. According to my own research, there has been a significant increase in the frequency of predatory black bear attacks in the last nine years. But most people are unaware of this increase and have not adjusted their attitudes in the way they deal with black bears.

It's quite common for black bears to be curious about people and approach for a better look. Some of these situations may be a mild form of predatory interest, but it's hard to tell. All predators have to carefully assess potential prey to make sure that they are not injured in the kill attempt. Most black bears probably have opportunistic predatory behaviour, but in many areas of North America they have significantly modified behaviour towards humans.

This is manifest by each generation of sows teaching their cubs to fear human sounds, smell, appearance, and often to be primarily nocturnal. This modified behaviour is probably responsible for the low frequencies of predatory attacks by black bears in some areas. There is also a lower frequency of these types of attacks in areas of major agricultural activity, probably because of the mortality inflicted on predatory bears by ranchers, farmers, conservation officers, etc. In contrast, there are places in the North where most black bears do not know what humans are.

On many occasions I have had young black bears approach me in what appeared to be a purely curious mode. But they must not be trusted because their mode can change quickly, and surviving a predatory encounter without injury requires quickly dissuading the bear before contact is made.

Most predatory encounters with black bears start with the bear following its prey, then circling closer, then a rush-charge, knockdown, and attempted kill. Sometimes black bears will drop their head and come straight for their prey in a slow, crouched walk (like Scott Whittemore's experience in the _Predacious Encounters and Attacks_ chapter). In most cases they are not doing bluffing displays or showing anger, but they may make some low growls. There have been a few progressive-predatory attacks by partially habituated black bears who were showing mild anger as they approached a person for camp food, then decided that the person was on the menu.

It is extremely important to continue to face a predatory bear and _maintain eye contact_. The bear is waiting for you to turn and run, as it is much less dangerous for them to take you from behind. Most predators have this chase response behaviour.

Consider all black bear encounters as having the potential to turn predatory. DON'T BE CARELESS WITH BLACK BEARS.

I am often asked by field workers what they should do when they see a bear at long range. I don't have a good answer for this question. If a person is unarmed, leaving the area is probably the wisest thing to do. But in some areas of the province there are now so many bears that daily multiple sightings are the norm during certain times of the year, and if you're working outdoors the day's work must still get done.

Most of the people who have had serious encounters leave an area where they see a bear. Some people who carry spray will watch a bear to see if it is leaving the area before they decide whether to leave or not. I have had mixed results yelling at bears to let them know I was there; some leave, some approach. If you are alone and not carrying a firearm - be cautious.

PARK ENCOUNTERS

The year 1992 was bad for bear attacks in National Parks. A hiker was killed and partially eaten by a sow grizzly with two cubs in Glacier National Park. A British tourist was severely mauled and her husband killed and partially eaten by a large male grizzly in Jasper Park. Two hikers from Seattle were mauled by a bear in Yoho National Park and one of them lost his right eye.

In the first two attacks, neither playing dead nor fighting back would have helped the victims, and in the third attack the people involved couldn't determine what the proper response should be, as the following account from *Canadian Press* will illustrate:

Hiking trail closed after bear attack
Hiker injured in encounter in Yoho Park

An American tourist attacked a bear with his

camera as the animal mauled his friend on a day hike in Yoho National Park.

Parks officials immediately closed the Lake O'Hara area, 18 kilometres east of Field, and evacuated hikers following the attack Friday.

The mauling occurred as two couples from Seattle were hiking on a trail above the mountain lake, 160 kilometres west of Calgary.

Peter Block, in his 30s, was flown by helicopter to Calgary's Bow Valley Centre, where he was in serious condition Saturday with puncture wounds and cuts to his upper body and head. John Gerstle, 55, was recovering from lacerations and puncture wounds at Banff's Mineral Springs Hospital.

The two men and their wives had been hiking in the area since Wednesday. Gerstle said Block was ahead of him on the trail when the bear charged his friend and knocked him to the ground.

"I thought it was a black bear, and I have been told with a black bear you have to fight them, so I started to hit it with my camera," he said in an interview from his hospital bed.

Gerstle said the bear then lunged at him, dragging him down an embankment, where it bit his shoulders and arms and clawed his head.

"At that point I expected to die."

The bear suddenly let go of him and attacked Block again, Gerstle said.

He crawled up the embankment and yelled at his friend to play dead.

Moments later the animal ran off and the two women ran for help.

Jeff Anderson, acting superintendent of Yoho National Park, said park officials are searching the area for the bear, but didn't know if it was a black bear or a grizzly.

Experts say a dry spring and wet summer

depleted the berries and plants bears feed on, forcing them to roam farther and become bolder with humans.

Bears have been spotted on golf courses and one was removed from a Calgary park.

* * *

The two following accounts of bear attacks obtained from *Canadian Press* also happened in National Parks in 1992. In these two cases playing dead with a grizzly and fighting back with a black bear *did* work:

Playing dead saves cyclist from grizzly
July 13, 1992, Jasper Alberta (Canadian Press)

An 18-year-old riding a mountain bike in Jasper National Park was chased and attacked by a grizzly bear, wardens say.

Warren Van Asten was riding his mountain bike along a dirt trail a few kilometres northeast of his home in Jasper Friday when he came face-to-face with two bears, said acting chief warden John Taylor.

Van Asten got off his bike about five metres from the two bears and retreated into a grove of pine trees. The larger of the two bears chased him and began biting and mauling his arms and legs.

The teen saved himself by playing dead, said Taylor.

"Anybody who has been in the claws and mouth of a grizzly bear and lived to tell the tale is a lucky man," said Taylor.

"When someone plays dead the bear perceives the threat as no longer real."

After the attack, Van Asten stumbled to Lake Annette, a picnic campground about one

kilometre from the trail and summoned help.
He was flown by air ambulance to an Edmonton hospital where he is in good condition after
receiving treatment for tendon damage and
puncture wounds to his back, arms, and legs.

Wardens determined that the bear was acting
normal by attacking Van Asten, said Taylor,
who suspects the larger bear was a grizzly sow
protecting her cub. Wardens closed trails in
the area and aren't planning to move or shoot
the bear said Taylor.

Meanwhile, a 23-year-old Jasper man cycling
along the same trail where Van Asten had been
attacked got a scare Saturday morning when
he spotted a brown-colored bear.

The man, whom Taylor wouldn't name, dismounted and walked his bike through the forest, giving the bear a wide berth. He got back
on the trail 50 metres in front of the bear and
resumed pedalling.

The bear trotted to within 15 metres of the frantic cyclist before disappearing into the bush.

* * *

Jump into river beats bear attack
June 18, 1992, Banff Alberta (Canadian Press)

Two backpackers from Quebec dived into a
frigid mountain river near Banff to escape an
attacking black bear.

The bear, which mauled one of the men, was
killed later when it charged at park wardens.

Louis-Phillippe Audette, 23, of Hull, Que., was
admitted to hospital in Banff with ankle and
calf injuries.

"It grabbed my hand and leg and pulled me
down," Audette said.

"I was tired of being chewed up by the bear so I

decided to rise up, scream and look him in the eyes.

"He was so surprised, I had time to jump in the river."

Moments earlier Audette and his brother were chased from their tent in the attack at a back-country campsite six kilometres south of Banff.

The men swam down the Spray River until they reached a fire road. They were found by two passing mountain bikers who went for help.

Author's note: This gentleman saved his life by sitting up and screaming at the black bear, then running and jumping into the river. But as far as I can determine he did not know that he was supposed to fight back. He lucked out and did the right thing.

It's very interesting to note how few predatory black bear attacks have taken place in parks, like the one above. There may be something about black bear behaviour that reduces their predatory instinct during habituation. There have been many predatory attacks by grizzly bears in parks - usually taking place at night with people in tents. But the frequency of predatory attacks in parks by both species may well increase if the present trend to over-protect bears in parks and adjacent areas continues.

Bowron Lake Provincial Park is a canoeist's paradise. The outdoor traveller can canoe and portage between a series of lakes with spectacular beauty. Bowron has over 4000 visitors a year and has had its share of habituated black bears that specialize in taking backpacks away from people who are portaging canoes or camping. In recent years parks personnel have worked hard to reduce this problem by improving back country campground food storage facilities, by ticketing campers that don't follow the park rules, by transporting habituated bears to other areas, and by killing those bears that have become dangerous.

Last year (August 1993) a park ranger had to kill a young female grizzly in Bowron Park that repeatedly charged him. This bear had been harassing tourists for several months. I asked this ranger if he had information as to whether this grizzly became a problem because of careless food handling by park users, or if it was just a hungry bear that could smell food in people's packs. He said he did not know what had caused this bear to become dangerous so fast.

During the final drafting of this book a bear attack took place in Bowron Park that demonstrates how difficult some types of attacks can be to survive:

On the morning of June 10, 1994, Mateus Rupert and Claudia Garshamer were camped at the Lynx Creek camp site on Isaac Lake. Mateus, 26, is from Munich, Germany and serving an internship at Harbor View Hospital in Seattle, Washington. Claudia, his fiancé, was on vacation from Germany.

About 7:00 a.m. they were awakened by a black bear scratching on the tent. The bear immediately started tearing the tent apart and both people yelled vigorously to try to scare the bear away. The canoeists quickly found themselves trapped inside the tent with the bear starting to zero in on the shapes inside.

Claudia quickly got under her sleeping mattress for protection, but Mateus could not do so because the bear was standing on his. Mateus rolled on top of Claudia to give her additional protection and the bear started biting and clawing at his head and back. The bear now had Mateus exposed but Claudia was still trapped in the tent.

Mateus was screaming and suffering intense pain as the bear attempted to rip him apart. Claudia was able to enlarge a tear in the tent and escape from the deadly trap that she was in. Mateus yelled at her to open the hut (there was an old log cabin near the campsite) that they had stored their backpacks in for the night. As Claudia raced for the old cabin she could hear her loved one screaming and crying for help as the bear was now tearing off chunks of flesh from Mateus' left leg.

Claudia saw an old worn-out ax near the cabin and without hesitation grabbed it and headed back to the tent. The bear was dragging its screaming victim into the bush when Claudia whacked it on the back of the neck. The bear instantly dropped Mateus and ran off. Mateus had given up hope and thought that he would soon suffer a slow agonizing and painful death.

The severely mauled young man crawled to the cabin with his mate helping him as best as she could. Once inside the cabin Claudia dressed his wounds, gave him water, and lit a fire. Mateus' leg wound was deep and bleeding heavily so Claudia decided that she must go for help and set about securing the cabin in case the bear came back.

When she stepped outside, the bear was back to the tent and licking it. She threw a chunk of wood and hit the bear, causing it to run off again. Mateus latched the door as Claudia ran for the canoe. She paddled with all her might down the lake towards the ranger station at the other end.

Claudia was not gone long before Mateus could hear the bear circling the cabin.

The bear scratched the window and although Mateus didn't think he could stand up, he forced himself to do so, and hit the logs near the window with the ax. The bear ran off again as Mateus fainted and collapsed to the floor. When he came to he forced himself to get up and push the table against the door. The bear came back and once again searched for weak spots in the exterior of the cabin.

As Claudia paddled along she found herself in mental torment. Had she made the right decision, or should she have tried to bring Mateus along with her in the canoe. Would the bear return and get into the cabin? She had traveled for several hours and was close to her objective when she saw two park rangers in a motorboat. She flagged them down and related the bear attack incident. After a helicopter was summoned, Claudia and the rangers sped back to the campsite, arriving at 10:45 a.m. The couple was air-lifted to G.R. Baker Memorial Hospital in Quesnel, B.C.

Conservation officers were flown in and worked with park personnel to trap and kill the bear. It was later determined that the campers did not have food in their tent and had followed all park rules.

Even though Mateus required 300 stitches to be closed up, and was at first listed in critical condition, he was soon stable enough to be flown to the hospital in Seattle where he soon recovered. Claudia is reluctant to be acclaimed as a hero, but hopefully she realizes that many people would have been hopelessly paralyzed in that same situation.

Author's note: The parks personnel who dealt with this attack seemed to have a fairly realistic view of this incident, but there were the usual statements by other Ministry of Environmental employees as to how "rare" this type of behaviour was and also that there might have been something wrong with the bear. There were also the usual statements about people being careless with garbage.

I'm sure that every reader of this book recognizes this story as a clear-cut predatory attack and a type of behaviour that is not as "rare" as some people would have us believe. It is quite possible that the bear involved in this episode had no prior experience with people because Bowron Park has a very narrow circular corridor of human use. There is often an attempt to blame people for bear attacks.

If you are planning a camping trip in a park that has bears, your statistical risk of being attacked is very low. But you will enjoy your trip more, and sleep better, if you follow these guidelines.

A tent is a very important defensive device in a park, not as a physical barrier, but because it confuses most bears. The bear will usually circle several times, letting you know it is there. This gives you time to use a defensive measure. Each person in the tent must have a can of bear spray, a flashlight, and a good knife in a scabbard (with a fixed 5" blade - not a folding knife) if they are going to survive a nighttime predatory attack. These items should be on each person's side of the tent.

Once you are aware of the bear near the tent, and it is away from the door, one person should unzip the door flap part-way, hold it open, and shine the light through it to blind the bear. The other person should spray the bear as soon as it comes into view. If you do not have a chance to open the door and the bear starts attacking the tent, one person should keep the light pointed towards the bear and the other person slit the tent with a knife, then spray the bear as soon as you see its nose. Under these circumstances you will get spray on yourself and will be forced to vacate the tent shortly thereafter. Keep the can of spray in your hand while leaving the tent if possible. Sometimes a bear will tear the tent open and you can spray it when you see its head. If a bear ends up standing on, and biting a person through the tent, the other person must get outside and spray the bear. You may have to use the knife to cut your way out, or use it to stab the bear. Try to keep your cool, and don't give up.

DON'T HIKE OR CAMP IN ANY PARK WITHOUT BEAR SPRAY.

NEVER SLEEP IN THE OPEN IN A PARK.

Never feed a bear under any circumstances, and dissuade a bear that is approaching your camp from coming any closer as soon as possible.

Follow all park rules about food storage, camp set-up, etc., but still expect a possible bear encounter. Be ready.

If you encounter a bear on a trail, follow the encounter strategy guidelines in the *Encounter Survival Strategy* chapter. If you encounter a bear that is aware of you, indifferent to you, and at a safe distance, and you want to photograph it, ready your defense system, stay where you are, and photograph the bear. Then back off slowly or watch the bear until it leaves the area. DO NOT APPROACH THE BEAR.

ATTACK SURVIVAL

Whenever you work or play in remote areas you need an evacuation plan and if possible a communication system. When I go hunting in wild areas I leave a map with my wife that shows travel routes and proposed camp locations. I make a notation on the map of the day I'll be back with the instructions to have a helicopter fly the map routes if I don't show up.

An employee who works for the Ministry of Forests told me a story about a black bear that kept approaching her and forcing her down a hill-side. She felt she had been saved because she had a hand radio and she called the helicopter pilot who had dropped her off and who was fueling up the machine just over the hill.

The pilot quickly got the helicopter in the air and chased the bear off just in time. She felt that the bear had been acting predaciously.

Even if you are out for just a day trip, you should have a day pack with survival gear and a first aid kit. Most first aid kits do not have enough large compress bandages for serious wounds; you need a 3", 4", and 6" compress in your gear, and two elasticized wrap bandages.

8

Encounter Survival Strategy

I have come to the opinion that there are three different bear behavioural modes in relation to encounters with humans: wild, man-wise, and habituated. Wild bears do not have a learned fear of humans but in some circumstances will retreat from the unknown. Man-wise bears have learned fear of humans either from their mother, direct experience, or both. Habituated bears are not fearful of people and come in a variety of types. Some are habituated to human presence but not human food or garbage; others are habituated to both. Some are not aggressive; some are very aggressive.

Coming up with simple strategies that will handle both species, all behavioural modes, and endless varying circumstances, is a supreme challenge. We will never completely eliminate death and injury from bear attacks, but we can significantly improve on present concepts about bear encounter strategies. In general, there are three broad categories of bear attacks:

Defensive-aggressive: The bear feels that you are a threat and will try to bluff you away; if necessary, it will make contact, immobilize you, then retreat.

Predatory: The bear is stalking you as prey and will try to kill and eat you.

Unknown behaviour: This is the sticky wicket category. It has been increasing in frequency during recent years and in 1992 came forward as a major problem. I am lumping many sub-categories into this class of attack, but they all have the same problem: Neither playing dead with grizzlies, nor fighting back (bare-handed) with black bears will work. In some of these sub-categories the person involved cannot determine species or behaviour.

These sub-categories are not based on what the final outcome of an event was; rather, could the person involved have determined the attack category and therefore the appropriate response?

Unknown behaviour sub-categories:

1. A bear is approaching people and they cannot determine which species it is.
2. A bear is approaching people showing some anger.
3. Extremely aggressive predatory black bears (probably starved).
4. Extremely aggressive predatory grizzly bears.
5. Sow grizzly encounters with second-year cubs that follow her lead (could be defensive-aggressive or predatory).
6. Progressive-predatory where the bear seems defensive-aggressive at first, then switches to a predatory mode.

These sub-categories I have chosen are based not only on the published recent bear attacks but also on some of the many bear encounter stories I have heard. Unfortunately the aggressive behaviour of both species is much too complex for simple strategies to work.

Many government ministries are presently trying to up-date their bear encounter information pamphlets. They are generally taking the simplified version of Herrero's strategy (play dead with grizzlies and fight back with black bears) as the final response when contact seems imminent. When I first developed my bear hazard safety course in 1989, I changed this strategy to "play dead in a defensive-aggressive attack and fight back in a predatory attack" when contact seems imminent. I told people to base their decision on behaviour, not species. This was an attempt to resolve the problem that these attack categories do not split 100% between the two species, and also to resolve the problem of many people being unable to distinguish between the two species. I believe this was an improvement, but after completing my three studies mentioned in the *Introduction*, I stopped recommending this strategy unless a person has no other choice.

I am including the following two stories in order to make sure that you understand two of the main points of this book: *There are many encounters and attacks taking place that most biologists and governments do not know about, and a good portion of them are of a type that the person involved could not possibly determine what the proper unarmed strategy should be.*
When reading these accounts, put yourself in the person's boots and try to determine what strategy you would have used in the situation if you were unarmed. Remember, these people did not have the luxury of looking back on the event and knowing all factors of the story. They had to make a quick judgment based only on the information available:

Subject: June 14/85 Kimsquit Bear Encounter
Attention: Mid Coast Forest District
O. H. & S. Committee

Remarks: Background - on June 14/85 (a.m.)

Jim Hall (Doman Industries Ltd., Area Eng.), Ken Dunsworth (B.C.F.S., Zone Tech.) & Otto Pflanz (R.O. Engineering B.C.F.S.) were conducting a ground reconnaissance of proposed road and falling boundary locations for Block 52 within Robson Valley of the Kimsquit watershed. Jim Hall was carrying a 30-06 calibre rifle for "bear protection". Although the weapon had a sling, he carried it in hand, muzzle down; in addition there was a cartridge in the chamber, with the safety on (we were all aware of this prior to setting out). It should be noted at this point that Mr. Hall has extensive shooting and hunting experience.

No member of the party was carrying a bell or noise maker. It was raining heavily so all party members were wearing raingear, in fact Mr. Dunsworth had his hood pulled over his hard hat. A road construction crew was working approximately 1.25 km from the site of the encounter. During the two hours prior to the encounter the lead was traded a number of times in no planned or set manner.

After walking the mainline through to the end of Block 52, we walked up to the backline of 52 and started angling uphill and down-valley. Timber in the area was mature (no low limbs), sideslopes were 70%-90%, a number of streams were encountered, and the terrain was very "bluffy".

Due to terrain, heavy timber, and brush, we were not aware of the slide track until we had come out of the gully just west of it. The creek in the gully was in relatively high flow and therefore very noisy. Upon coming out of the gully Pflanz looked forward, caught a glimpse of a black bear, and called out "Bear"! (Only the head was visible above the lip of the slide track.) As the bear came running over the lip of the slide track, Pflanz called out "Bear" again. At this time Hall began to raise the rifle to his shoulder. As Dunsworth had not reacted to the first two warnings, Pflanz called out "Bear, he's coming". The bear, still running, was 3-4 metres ahead of Dunsworth at this point. At that time Dunsworth sited the bear, turned 180° and moved past Hall and Pflanz on the downhill side. Immediately upon Dunsworth clearing the line of sight Hall took his rifle off safety and fired at the bear, striking it in its left shoulder. The bear turned downhill and disappeared from view.

All of the foregoing took three to five seconds.

After approximately 30 seconds of looking, the bear was sighted about 15 metres downhill from us. Its movement was erratic. Hall fired a second shot, downing the bear. A third insurance shot was fired into the bear's head. Upon examination the bear was found to be a lactating female. After a short search of the area a large cub was found ten metres up a tree.

In order to determine whether the cub was old enough to fend for itself, Dunsworth and Pflanz sought out Tony Hamilton of Fish and Wildlife branch who was doing a Grizzly Bear study in the Kimsquit and they returned to the site. The attack was discussed with Mr. Hamilton who is an expert on bears. Mr. Dunsworth commented that as the bear was running towards him, its eyes were so wide open the white portion around the fringes of the eyes was visible and its ears were laying flat. After describing the incident to Hamilton he commented that the charge was not a bluff or warning; the bear was "committed" to carrying out the attack. There was no auditory or visual warning that we were aware of. The bear may have made some threatening noises but due to the rushing of the creek they would have been impossible to hear. Mr. Hamilton made the comment that on rare occasions a bear will attack with no warning.

Consequences - fortunately none of the people involved were injured. This incident could very easily have ended in a fatality. Had a member of the group not been carrying a firearm and been fully prepared, one can only guess what would have happened, as there were no climbable trees in the area and the terrain did not lend itself to a hasty retreat.

Another hazard brought to light in all of this was our attitude towards the firearm in our midst. The gun was along for the ride. While hunting, the man with the gun would never have been in the middle.

Recommendations - training should be provided to mid coast field staff on the subject of assessing bear hazard, avoiding bear incidents, and what to do when confronted by a bear.

Field staff should be provided with and required to carry noise making devices (bells etc.) when in the bush. (Due to terrain and background noise it is doubtful whether the bear, in our case, would have been alerted any earlier.)

It should be emphasized that when in the field in the company of a firearm, staff members *must* be constantly aware of *the gun* along with the ever-changing degree of bear hazard encountered.

Author's note: When the above three gentlemen left their vehicle they had a discussion over whether the gun should be carried with a shell in the chamber or not. Jim Hall was determined to do so, because six months previous his head chainman had been severely mauled by a grizzly.

Otto Pflanz and Ken Dunsworth still work in the mid coast area. Neither of them enjoy the thought of having to kill a bear, but both have been taking my firearms training for years and will defend themselves vigorously, if necessary.

* * *

Black Bear Attack
Near Vanderhoof, B.C.
September 10, 1992
by Vince Sewell

On opening morning of the 1992 moose season, Mike Pritchard and I were hunting near Vanderhoof in a large patch of bush. The area had been logged about 10-15 years ago and is full of old roads. The bush is a mixture of openings, deciduous cover, and immature pine, which is perfect cover for moose, deer, and other animals.

Mike and I split up at daybreak with him going to hunt the south half of the area and I was going to cover the northern portion. I walked along several of the old roads always trying to hunt into the wind. At about 7:30 a.m. I was working my way along a road which ran through thick patches of aspen and openings when I spotted a black bear feeding on some rose hips about 45-50 metres ahead of me. I stopped and stood still knowing that the bear couldn't see me because of my camouflage.

In the next few seconds I spotted three more bears, which turned out to be large cubs feeding near the sow, but all on the far side of her. At this point in time I decided to try to back away without being seen. Just as I was going to move

I felt the wind switch and blow right from me to
the bears. The sow lifted her nose to sniff, then
dropped and came at me at a fast lope. I yelled
to try to stop her but that just pinpointed my location to her, and she came even faster.

She never made any sounds or gave any indi-
cation that she was bluffing. As soon as I realized that she would not stop, I raised my rifle
and shot her. She dropped immediately about
30 metres away and didn't move. I wasn't sure
where I had hit her but found out later it was just
above the right eye. Because I wasn't sure that
she would stay down, I walked up within about
20 metres of her to see if she was dead. As I
stood there one of the cubs walked over and
looked at her, but moved away when I yelled.
The cubs were very large and I thought that they
were last year's cubs, but later learned that they
were still nursing.

As the cubs moved back a fifth bear, a large
boar, came out of the trees about 40 metres away
and started walking towards her. I wanted to
scare the boar away and to make sure that the
sow would not get up again so I fired another
shot into the sow. The boar never even hesi-
tated but walked right up to her and smelled the
blood. At this time I backed slowly away
because I didn't want to kill any other bears
and I only had three shells left, and there was
still four bears. The boar watched me go but
didn't attempt to follow or charge. I made a
large circle around the bears and met up with
Mike. He said that he had plenty of shells so we
walked back to get the bear I had shot.

When we arrived at the scene the cubs were all
standing over the sow but backed off as we
approached. As we were standing by the sow
looking at her the boar came out of the bush
about 40 metres away. When we yelled he

stopped and went about five feet up a tree where he hung snorting and growling at us. He then dropped to the ground and took a few steps toward us, then stopped. He just stood there watching and growling at us for a couple of minutes, then took another couple of steps towards us. We both feel that he almost charged several times, and if only one of us had been there, he would have charged. We didn't want to shoot him if we didn't have to; finally he backed off and disappeared into the bush. About a minute later we heard him again and could tell that he was trying to circle around us. We wanted to clean out the sow but didn't dare put our rifles down because the boar was still so close and so aggressive.

At this time we decide to go get an ATV to carry the bear out to where it could be safely cleaned and skinned. When we returned about an hour later there were no bears in sight, but the sound of the engine must have chased them away as they had cleaned up all the blood. When we skinned the sow we could see that she was very fat and her stomach was full. She also still had a very small amount of milk.

Possible factors in the attack:
Cubs - they were on the far side of her and I was no threat to them.
Food - possible but they were eating rose hips and berries and this was a good year for them, at least in this bush patch.
Boar - possible that having a boar around her cubs made her aggressive and having me on the scene was just too much for her, but she appeared to be fairly relaxed when I first saw her.

Or maybe it was combination of the above

factors. I don't feel that this was a predatory attack because she did not appear to be hungry, but at the same time the bears are trying to fatten up prior to denning. We also found the aggressive behaviour of the boar strange. I have no doubt that had I been unarmed I would have been killed.

Author's note: This story really demonstrates the unpredictability in bear behaviour in relation to not knowing what has just gone on prior to an encounter. At least a third of the encounter stories I have heard are similar to the ones above; like the three engineers who dropped their packs to distract a rapidly advancing black bear, and were shocked when it scrambled over their discarded offerings and kept up its pursuit; or the two cruisers who spent eight hours up a spindly hemlock looking down at a menacing grizzly that alternated between trying to push the tree over and sleeping. Like one of these gentleman told me: "It just ain't no fun swinging back and forth six feet while clinging to a sapling by your toenails and looking down on a monster with ten-inch fangs, all the time praying that the tree doesn't have root-rot."

* * *

UNARMED DEFENSIVE STRATEGIES

Tree climbing: This can be an effective strategy in some cases, but there are also cases where bears have climbed up and yanked people down. Black bears are very effective at climbing trees. Even though grizzly bears lose their ability to climb with their claws in the fourth year of their life, some adult grizzlies can climb trees quite well, particularly if the tree is medium size (30-60cm) and has strong limbs. Do not climb a tree during a bear encounter if you have a spray for defense. Stand behind the tree and spray the bear at about three metres or closer.

I have heard several successful accounts of people surviving bear attacks by climbing trees. But in each case the person broke off a limb or took off a jacket while in the tree, or took a limb up the tree with them and then beat the tree and yelled when the bear started up, or hit the bear when it got close. In one case the black bear started up three times before backing off. If you kick the bear under these circumstances, hang on tight, aim for the nose, and retract your foot quickly.

Water: This can be a good defense under some circumstances. Several times I have stood on the edge of the Atnarko River contemplating a quick dive if the sow got any closer. It must be a good size river or lake, and you must start swimming immediately and get some distance.

Backpacks: On many occasions backpacks have saved people from a more serious injury or death. If you can keep the backpack between you and the bear during an attack, do so. A dropped pack may distract some bears, but not all bears.

DEFENSIVE DEVICES

Airhorns: These and other loud noise makers are important bear avoidance devices and should be deployed often when cover, noise, or wind conditions dictate. But they should not be considered a defense item. Use deep low-pitched horns only.

Flares: Flares have basically been proven as an unreliable tool for deterring bears. They have been banned in some places because of their potential for starting fires. But I have heard several stories where flares deterred bears.

Bear bangers: These devices propel a projectile that explodes at a certain distance. I have talked to many people who have used these and it seems that they work successfully about half the time. Sometimes

the projectile goes past the bear, then explodes - and
here comes the bear in the wrong direction.

Most experienced people shoot bear bangers straight
up into the air. But sometimes the bear still runs in
the wrong direction. What's more, some bears are
not afraid of bangers. Don't stake your life on bear
bangers. They are worth carrying, and they work
some of the time, but don't consider them as a defensive system.

Pepper spray deterrence: In the mid 1970s Charles
Jonkel, of the University of Montana, and a Montana businessman, Bill Pounds, developed a bear
spray that later became know as Counter Assault.
They experimented with several types of chemicals,
and it eventually became clear that Oleoresin Capsicum, a derivative of cayenne pepper, was the best
chemical for deterring bears.

Since that time, many other companies have developed and marketed sprays for bear, dog, and human
deterrents. Some products have come and gone; currently there are four brands of pepper bear spray reg-
istered with the Pest Control Branch of Agriculture
Canada: Assault-Guard Bear Repellent, Bear Guard
Deterrent, Phazer For Bears, and Bear Scare. Counter Assault has temporarily withdrawn their product
from the Canadian market because of the chlorofluo-
rocarbon (C.F.C.) ban that came into effect last year.
This was unfortunate because this product, containing C.F.C., had the best propellent and penetrated
wind farther. Some of the other products have a
higher percent of Capsicum, or higher burn rating
than Counter Assault, but Counter Assault has been
used longer and has the most cases of successful
defense. I have never sprayed a bear, but I have done
wind and volume testing with Bear Guard, Counter
Assault, and Phazer. Counter Assault and Bear
Guard are the most popular brands in B.C., but I have
confidence in all three. Counter Assault is probably
the most widely distributed spray in Canada.

Retailers must keep records of purchasers of bear sprays because it is a restricted product in Canada, and it is against the law to use it against anything other than what is stated on the label. Dog sprays are also available.

Pepper spray does not come close to firearms as a defense system, but in the last seven years there have been enough cases of people successfully deterring attacking bears in the wild to consider these products beyond the experimental stage. The following example illustrates this:

On the morning of April 22, 1992, Dan Balwin started the day off badly when he fell in the river. Dan lived in Prince George, B.C. and worked for E. P. Runtz and Associates who were doing contract engineering for North Wood Pulp and Timber. They were working near Pass Lake, east of Prince George, at the time.

The river was about half way to the bottom of the cut-block; after Dan drained his boots and wrung out his clothes, he and Gene, a co-worker, proceeded the remaining three kilometres. At the bottom boundary they split up. Gene started marking the boundary line and Dan ran a deflection line up the center of the block. It was close to noon when Dan reached the top boundary. He marked about 200 metres of the top line and decided to have lunch before starting his second deflection line back down the hill.

Both men were working on snowshoes as there was still over a metre of snow on the ground. Dan picked the base of a large spruce tree where the snow had melted back for a lunch spot; this gave him a nice view of the hill-side below. He was half-way through a sandwich when he noticed a grizzly emerge from the

timber into a small opening 40 metres below
him. At first Dan thought the bear might go
right past him, but the bear stood up on its hind
legs and started sniffing the air. All of a sudden Dan realized that the bear was down-wind
from him and knew that he was there somewhere. Dan grabbed his pack to locate his bear
bangers but remembered that he had lost them
in the river.

Two days before this incident Dan had an
encounter with a grizzly; the two of them stood
facing each other at ten metres for a couple of
minutes before the bear left peaceably. This
had frightened Dan so he obtained some Counter Assault bear spray the next day. He had
stopped carrying a firearm about two years previously but didn't really have much confidence in the spray.

Dan remembered the bear spray and removed
it from his pack. When he looked back down
the hill, things had gotten worse; there were
now three bears - a sow and two large cubs -
and they were starting up the incline towards
him. Dan made a quick decision to yell at the
sow, hoping she would turn away, but this gave
her his location and she started lunging
through the snow directly at him.

Dan readied the can of spray but had a gut-
wrenching feeling come over him; he didn't
know if the spray would work, and he was
afraid that the sow and two cubs must have been
hunting him predaciously. The sow was on top
of him in seconds, but she had to slow down at
the last instant because Dan was sitting with
his back against the tree. The two cubs were
behind and off to the side as the sow attacked;
her claws were just one foot from the tips of
Dan's snowshoes when he pushed the lever on
the spray (later confirmed by tracks in the

snow).

Her front legs buckled, and she went down immediately. For an instant she was stunned, but just as quickly as she had come, she spun around and galloped down the hill-side with the cubs right behind. Dan thought to himself that this was too easy; she would probably come back. He waited about ten minutes, watching and listening, then dashed for the river.

Author's note: The reason that the sow went down was not just because of the blinding or burning effect of the spray; it was the nerve-shock to the respiratory tracts and the immediate asphyxiation caused by asperated capsicum. Now that propellents for bear spray cannot have C.F.C.s in them, the fine misting of the chemical is reduced, and the important aspiration effect is reduced as well.

While Dan's experience with pepper spray was successful, there are problems with spray deterrents that make it critical that the user know how to use it properly. In a 16 km cross-wind, the spray will only go about two-and-a-half metres before drifting sideways. If you are spraying down-wind, it will go six-eight metres before dispersing too much to be effective. If you tried to spray a predatory black bear that was up-wind from you at about eight metres with 20 km gusts, the spray would turn right around at about three-and-a-half metres and come back on you. You would immediately be asphyxiated, blinded, and burning all over. The bear would probably enjoy the pepper seasoning on his lunch.

The information on the can says to manoeuvre the bear down-wind. This may sound ridiculous, but there are some predatory attacks where this may be possible. If you can move cross-wind and get behind, or against a large rock, or tree, do so. It will help control the direction the bear will come from, and possibly slow down its final approach.

There are, of course, some encounters, like Dan Balwin's, where you would just have only enough time to get the can out of the holster and spray the bear at very close range.

Pepper spray is a close-range deterrent system and you may get some spray on yourself, but if you can deliver a two or three second burst on a bear's face at three or four metres, you will see an immediate reaction. If you had a bear approach you down-wind, or if wind was not a problem, there would be nothing wrong with giving a one-second burst at the eight metre range; this would stop some bears. Note that there are only about ten, one-second bursts of spray in a can. This is plenty to deter a bear, but not if you waste it trying to spray a bear circling at ten metres. Wait until the bear is three metres or closer before spraying.

The product should be considered a temporary deterrent. If you stopped the bear but did not get a real good dose on its face, the bear may come back. Leave the area immediately. I have a recent report from Jim Hart, the District Conservation Officer (C.O.) in Fort Nelson, B.C. He states that some of the problem black bears along the Alaskan Highway that have been repeatedly sprayed by C.O.s or Parks staff become somewhat resistant to spray, and return to the area quickly.

If you are serious about spray deterrents, you should buy three cans: One for testing during wind conditions so you will clearly understand its limitations, and two for carrying on your belt. With a can in each hand, you have a significantly increased deterrent power. Two or three people using sprays together is a formidable defense. Practice getting the can out of the holster quickly.

Pepper spray should be issued, stored, and handled as a weapon. Never leave it in a vehicle over winter or store it where it will be subjected to extreme cold. Take care of it, and it will take care of you.

Bear sprays are dangerous if you have an accidental discharge in a vehicle or aircraft. Spray should be transported in a sealed container. You can make a spray container out of three-inch ABS plastic drain pipe and fittings. Whenever flying tell the pilot you're carrying bear spray.

I do not recommend a test spray burst from a can that you are going to carry, as suggested on some labels. I have two reports of cans (that had test bursts) losing their pressure when tested again months later. Replace your spray after three years, and use the old cans for test spraying.

Pepper spray is not recommended for use by people with respiratory problems.

If you plan to bring a pepper spray into Canada, contact Canadian Customs for information on the subject, as some products are illegal in Canada.

FIREARMS DEFENSE

In the last 29 years, I have killed many bears at close range; some were very large, and some were coming full-tilt. I have tested over 2,000 rounds of various types of rifle, shotgun, and handgun ammunition in wood and wallboard mediums. I have examined many wound channels in bears and recovered the bullets that made them. I have carefully studied what goes wrong with firearms and people when they are facing a dangerous bear.

In a normal bear defense situation, and excluding hunting of grizzlies at close-range, a person who is proficient with a large calibre rifle or pump 12-guage shotgun can reduce the risk of injury or death during a bear attack to about nil. Of course, the key point is firearms proficiency, and that means different things to different people. No matter how good you are, if you hunt grizzlies, or guide grizzly hunters, you will sooner or later have some close calls - usually while following up a wounded bear, or accidentally bumping into a sow with cubs, or walking up to a bear with a carcass that you don't know is there. Occasionally a black bear will scare the hell out of a hunter as well.

Any good-quality rifle that you are very familiar with and does not jam, that has 30-06 power and up, will do the job in all but the rarest of cases. High-quality ammunition with heavier thick-skinned bullets are needed - for example, Federal Premium with Nosler partition bullets, or Remington ammunition with Swift a-frame bullets. If you load your own, Barnes X are good bullets that will smash large bones without disrupting too badly.

In the last five years, I have seen thousands of rounds put through defense pump shotguns during range exercises. These shotguns are problematic and if your operational techniques aren't just right, they will jam. I have met people who didn't believe this until I put them through one of my range exercises designed to simulate bear attack stress. If you are an experienced shotgun user and you get your techniques down pat, then a 12-gauge pump shotgun is a fast, powerful firearm.

Some people do not consider shotguns adequate for bear defense. The secret is in the ammunition. Never use buckshot; it might kill a grizzly at 12 metres, and it might not. Federal 1-1/4 oz. magnum slugs are what you need, plus a shoulder pad that fits under your clothing.

The only shotgun that I would recommend, at this time, is the Remington 870 police model with a three-inch chamber. It must have a 20" barrel with rifle sights, and it must be shot accurately, just like a rifle. Some of the Remington 870s that have been manufactured in the last three years have jamming problems, or they only work well with 3" ammunition. Make sure you thoroughly range-test any defense weapon. Get yourself a set of 12-gauge ammunition dummies and practice with them until

you make no mistakes. NEVER PUT 3" AMMUNI-
TION IN A 2-3/4" CHAMBER.

If you can legally carry a handgun and your work
necessitates it, then a .44 magnum is minimum. A
.357 magnum will not do the job on a frontal charging grizzly. Practice double-handed, single-action
shooting at 25 metres for accuracy, and double-action
shooting at ten metres. If you can't consistently put
most of your rounds into a six-inch bull's-eye, then
carry a rifle or shotgun. Once you decide to pull the
trigger on a bear, you must kill it quickly.

Always carry your spare ammunition in the same
place, and practice pulling it from that place when
you do shooting practice.

Advanced safety: It took me 20 years to develop the
advanced safety and weapons use procedures that I
teach in my firearms courses. The system of training I use is completely different than other systems,
and is specialized for defense against bears. It has a
component that demonstrates what goes wrong with
firearms and people in a defense situation.

The advanced safety aspect is based on the fact that
most accidental firearm discharges happen near a
camp, vehicle, or boat, and usually when a person is
loading or unloading a gun or carrying a firearm
with a shell in the chamber. Another dangerous situation is during and shortly after a bear encounter.

My procedures are too complicated to explain here,
but I will give you some do's and don'ts:

1. You cannot be safe with a firearm that you
are not completely familiar with. Practice
often.

2. Make sure there are no obstructions in the
barrel by sliding a cleaning rod down it.
Always put tape over the end of your barrel
before going into the field.

3. Never cycle rounds through a chamber when
loading or unloading. This is the number one

killer. You can devise a system for almost any firearm for unloading without cycling rounds through the chamber.

4. NEVER CARRY A ROUND IN THE CHAMBER. Put one in only when you are ready to fire, or when danger is imminent. If the danger is temporarily over and you need to keep a round in the chamber, put your safety on, bring the barrel straight up, and keep your thumb or a finger on the safety. De-chamber as soon as the danger is over.

5. Never fire unless you are sure of what your target is.

6. As soon as a bear incident is over, tell everyone with a firearm to immediately put barrels straight up and remove chambered rounds.

7. Always be careful of where your barrel is pointing.

8. Keep your finger out of the trigger cage until ready to fire.

9. Keep the action open when your gun is unloaded.

10. Always transport and store firearms in a protective guncase with a trigger lock or action lock in place.

11. Be properly licenced, and obey all laws.

12. "Loaded firearm" in B.C. means ammunition anywhere in the gun.

WHEN TO KILL A BEAR

The most difficult question that I have had to deal with in my firearms training program is, "Under what conditions is it appropriate to kill a bear in self-defense?"

When I first developed my bear safety program I knew that I would have to answer that question decisively, or my program would fail. I also knew that no matter what defense guidelines I came up with, there would be some people who would not like my strategies. But let me make one thing crystal clear: My bear hazard safety program is a safety program for people first, and bears second.

If I had developed my bear defense guidelines after the first 15 encounters I had, they would have been substantially different. If I had developed them after the next ten encounters, they would have come out even more differently. But many encounters later, I was subjected to what I call the 5% behaviour. You have to have had many bear encounters and have studied their behaviour for years before you experience and recognize the types of encounters where there is high probability of the bear making contact.

The last person on earth that you want to take advice from about bear encounters is someone who has had a few encounters and assumes he has seen all the variations of bear aggressive behaviour. There is no doubt that my knowledge on this subject is not yet complete, but I don't expect any new information on this topic in the near future. No one is interested in it, and no one is going to spend 25 years of direct observation to detect these rare and subtle behavioural patterns.

Six years ago I carefully analyzed my own bear encounters, compared them to all published encounters and attacks, and came up with a group of encounter types where probability of contact is high. This is not to say that it is possible to determine that other more normal types of encounters won't end in contact, or that these particular types will always end with contact. That cannot be done. But we can recognize those types of encounters where the chance of contact is high, based on statistical probability.

There will be, of course, many encounters where the person involved cannot read what is going on, but in many encounters you will have a pretty good idea why the bear is acting like it is and what may happen next. The firearms defense guidelines that I propose are not perfect, and they are tipped in favor of people, but they give both people and bears a reasonable chance of survival. In my opinion, if a large number of people followed these guidelines over a long period of time, for every three bears shot, two would have made contact, and one not. But many people who have taken my course tell me that now that they know most bear encounters do not end in contact, and now that they understand bear aggressive behaviour better, they feel they are less likely to shoot a bear unnecessarily.

Anyone who carries a firearm for defense against bears has the responsibility to practice good avoidance procedure and must try to avoid close contact with bears.

You have the lawful right to defend your life and property against wild animals. This, of course, must be tempered with not killing animals unnecessarily. But once it is clear in your mind that you are endangered, defend yourself vigorously.

These suggested guidelines are designed to give a person time for at least one good shot in a worst-case-scenario, but I do not guarantee that a successful defense will always result:

75 metre guideline

At this range you must ready yourself for defense as some bears may choose fight over flight.

I do not believe in giving bears warning shots unless there are two people with firearms. I will not use up any of my defense rounds, or take the chance of jamming the next round. With two firearms, one person can stay defense ready and the other person can put warning shots ahead and slightly to the side of the bear.

25 metre guideline

At this range you shoot the bear:

1. If you have a grizzly encounter where first-year cubs go up a tree, second-year cubs follow, a sow charges from a long distance without bluffing, or you think a carcass is nearby.
2. In any family encounter (black or grizzly) where the distance between you and the cubs cannot be increased, or where cubs accidentally run towards you.
3. If you have a surprise close-range encounter with any bear, and the bear immediately charges (may or may not be showing anger).
4. If you feel you are seeing predatory behaviour by any bear.
5. If a bear comes at you in a low, crouched run.

If it is a straight frontal charge, shoot dead center of the body mass. If the bear is angling towards you, and you can make a point-of-the-shoulder shot, do so. The first shot is to immobilize the bear, then two quick follow-up shots to the center of chest (lungs), to bleed the bear to death.

It is your perogative to increase this defense distance as you feel it is required. But if you shoot a sow at 50 metres when the cubs have already started away from you, you are not giving her much of a chance. I'm not going to give you an absolute rule that may get you killed. These are guidelines and you must use your own discretion.

There are times when fisheries personnel walk up on grizzlies closer than 25 metres; in most of these cases the bear lets out a "whoooooff" and takes off away from the person. Do not shoot at the tail end of an escaping bear that is probably more terrified than you are.

If you shoot at, wound, or kill a bear, call the nearest Conservation Officer as soon as possible. Follow his

or her instructions as what to do. Do not remove anything from the bear before talking to a C.O. If you
are out in the bush, and it will be days before you can
contact authorities, try to warn anyone in the area
about the location of the carcass, as another bear may
soon be feeding on it. The carcass may have to be
removed from the area.

There are three possible levels of defense: firearms, bear spray, and unarmed. There is a difference in potential survival between the three. If three
different people were well trained in each of the levels, and they each had worst-case-scenario attacks, it
is my opinion (based on all information I presently
have) that the chance of coming through without serious injury or death is as follows: firearms 95%,
spray 70%, and unarmed 45%. Previously I was rating spray defense slightly higher (80%), but because
of the C.F.C. ban, I have lowered the rating.

ENCOUNTER STRATEGY GUIDELINES

It is not possible to devise a set of rules that will eliminate the chance of injury or death during bear attacks, but it is my opinion that the following guidelines create the best chance for survival:

GUIDELINE 1. Never expose yourself to bear attack hazard without a defensive system (spray or firearm).

GUIDELINE 2. Never play dead with any bear; always defend yourself (see important note below).

GUIDELINE 3. If the bear is showing anger (defensive-aggressive), ready your defense system, and if possible, back away slowly.

GUIDELINE 4. If a bear is stalking you (predatory), ready your defense system, maintain eye contact, and quickly chase it off by yelling, throwing rocks, beating pans together, etc.

GUIDELINE 5. If you can't determine what's going on, or if you want to boil this all down to one guideline only, ready your defense system, stand your ground quietly, and defend yourself.

Note: If your defense system fails, or if you are foolish enough to believe that it's not necessary to defend yourself against bears, you have no choice but to play dead in a defensive-aggressive attack, and fight back in a predatory attack - that is, if you are lucky enough to experience an attack that clearly falls into one of these two categories.

9

Attacks, Encounters, and Incidents

Some readers may be disappointed that I haven't incorporated more of my own bear encounters into this book. There is a good reason why I haven't.

This guide has been written in a semi-technical way in order to provide a fair and balanced presentation of bear aggression. I have carefully picked accurate stories that reflect the statistical information I have on this subject.

Over the years I have experienced a lot of grizzly bear aggression because of the types and extent of grizzly exposure that I have deliberately taken. If I related even an eighth of my bear experiences in this work through direct stories, it would slant this material in a biased way. It would make bears look more aggressive than they are. I have chosen to impart most of my knowledge in this book through indirect means. But we must not have all work and no play.

This chapter is intended to broaden your scope about human/bear conflict by providing a wide spectrum of bear episode stories. I'm also going to lighten up a bit and throw in some additional information based on my own experiences, so let's get this chapter off to a proper start with some information about my firearms training program, and an interesting bear story.

In February of 1992, I received a phone call from Ron Donnelly who is the silvicultural planner at the Fort Nelson District Office of the Ministry of Forests. Ron wanted me to put on a bear hazard safety training course for the district staff. They needed both a firearms course and a training session for their personnel who do not carry firearms. We settled on a week in late April.

The staff in Fort Nelson really took to my firearms range exercise, especially the moving target. After I put participants through a series of different shooting exercises, they finish up with several attempts at putting three shots into a moving target that comes straight towards them from 25 metres.

The moving target is constructed by suspending a cable over the tops of two eight-foot wooden A-frames that are 25 metres apart. The cable is anchored to metal ground rods about ten metres beyond the A-frames at each end. I hang a wooden frame box with a target on the front from two pulleys on the cable. A rope suspended under the cable by curtain rod hangers runs from the box target to a pulley on the back A-frame where the operator stands. The shooter stands between two flags just in front of the operator and the simulated bear can be pulled at different speeds to create different levels of stress.

Ron Donnelly is a soft-spoken, amiable kind of guy that you can't help but immediately like. But his mild nature is deceiving; his demeanor changes radically when he steps between the flags and faces the moving target with a rifle in his hands. He takes on a serious, determined composure, and for good reason. Consider the following story:

April 20, 1994

Dear Gary,

As per your request, here is a brief account of my black bear encounter which occurred on September 3, 1987. Although the actual attack is imprinted on my mind as clearly as if it happened yesterday, - I find (to my surprise) that some of the details leading up to the event are quite sketchy in my memory. I have never written anything down about this incident, so perhaps this is to be expected.

I had been on a hiking and exploring vacation by myself in the West Chilcotin area of B.C. Two days before I planned to head back to Fort Nelson I camped at the north end of the dry looking mountain range that sits just north of Chilko Lake. This mountain range is quite rugged, but gentles out a bit where I was camped.

I was up early the next morning and started up the hill-side towards alpine. I planned another day of hiking and exploring to finish off my vacation. It was deer season, and I had been unsuccessful on an earlier hunt that year, so I carried my .243 Mauser bolt-action rifle with me. I also had on a small daypack containing my lunch, raincoat, and a thermos of tea.

I had been hiking for about an hour when I came upon some fresh deer tracks. I put a shell in the chamber and pulled the big wing safety on. This was uncharacteristic of me as I had been raised around firearms and had been taught to only chamber a round when you are about to fire. I continued along the trail following the tracks until I was in sparse sub-alpine timber at about 5,000 feet elevation.

I was approaching a large thicket of alpine fir

when a dark blur erupted from the trees. Out of instinct I flinched away from whatever it was, and was then hit hard in the left shoulder. As I hit the ground on my back I realized that I was being attacked by a bear. I kicked out with my feet as hard as I could and the bear clamped onto one of my boots, then started shaking me. The bear had an awful smell. I remember being turned over part way onto my stomach, then flipped back onto my back again. At this point I realized that I still had my gun in my hand - I shoved the barrel up under the bear's head, pushed the safety off and pulled the trigger.

When the gun went off my first thought was that I had shot myself as there was so much blood on my feet and legs. I was instantly scrambling back away from the bear, on my side, with my rifle still in hand. It was several minutes before I could stand, but when I did, I quickly put the gun to my shoulder and waited to see if the bear was going to move. As soon as I knew it was dead my legs began to shake and I felt weak all over; but, I also felt a great sense of relief. I moved over to a small rock by the side of the trail and sat down. The bear looked to be about a 225 pounder.

I don't know how long I sat there shaking, but eventually it dawned on me that my rifle was still loaded. I was quite surprised to find that there were only two rounds left in the clip that had contained four. I looked around the bear and found two spent brass. Somehow I had fired twice, but to this day I do not remember the second shot.

I had a sore shoulder for about a month. As frightening as this attack was, maybe I'm lucky it happened as it prepared me for the years that I have worked in the Fort Nelson area where predatory black bear behaviour is common.

Ron Donnelly
Fort Nelson, B.C.

Author's note: This black bear was most likely a predatory bear and Ron would not have saved himself if he was not an expert with firearms. People are very lucky that most predatory black bears do not attack with stealth and from cover as this bear did. They usually take time to assess potential human prey and show themselves in the process.

The Ministry of Forests field personnel in Fort Nelson face a significant danger from predatory black bears in that area. But Ron Donnelly and the local Conservation Officer, Jim Hart, have done much to reduce that danger.

* * *

The *Lakes District News* at Burns Lake, B.C. was good enough to let me use the following news item from 1992:

Attacking grizzly gunned down
Prepared by Burns Lake Conservation Service.

On October 12, Jim Tourond from Francois Lake was guiding two moose hunters, Dan Prpich and Charlie Bray, near Poplar Lake approximately 80 km southwest of Burns Lake.

They were returning to their vehicle through thick brush after seeing nothing except calf moose tracks which they had crossed several times.

Jim was leading and noticed a dark object approximately 30 feet away. He saw the object move and removed his rifle from his shoulder and loaded a round into the chamber. In the next few seconds Jim had to shoot from the hip at a 300 kg grizzly bear charging him. Jim figured he hit the bear at less than 15 feet and had to jump aside as the wounded bear landed where he was standing. One of his hunters fired three more rounds into the bear at point blank range and the other hunter shot the bear in the head.

Jim checked the spot where he first saw the bear and found the whole carcass of a cow moose buried under a pile of moss, dirt, leaves, and sticks. Jim figured the cow moose may have been trying to protect her calf from the grizzly and was killed doing so. The bear was sleeping on the carcass because it was warm due to it decaying and it would also prevent other scavengers from eating the moose. The bear awoke, and charged to protect his kill. It was sheer luck that they came directly on the bear and that the bear was seen before it charged.

Jim called the Conservation Officers to report the kill as required by the Wildlife Act. The area was inspected by the officers and due to the remote location and poor condition of the bear hide, only the front claws were salvaged. The bear appeared to be old and a tooth was removed to determine its age. Jim returned to guiding the next day.

Author's note: If you ever walk up on a large male grizzly defending a carcass, you will only have seconds to respond, and you'll have to do everything right to survive. Large males attack differently than sows or sub-adults; the intruder is usually dispatched quickly by a blow from the right front paw, then ripped to shreds for insurance. The new carcass is then added to the decaying pile.

When I was young and didn't know better, I deliberately walked up on many grizzlies defending carcasses. In one such case I had a large male circling me, but he made the mistake of stepping on a small limb. If I hadn't heard that limb break, I probably wouldn't be sitting here now, writing this book.

* * *

Department of Fisheries (D.F.O.) personnel do "creek walks" on the B.C. Coast in order to obtain fish escapement numbers which are used for setting the commercial fishery openings for the following two or three weeks. I have heard a lot of negative statements about D.F.O. personnel killing bears unnecessarily. Twenty five years ago they did kill a lot of bears, and probably some unnecessarily.

During the last four years of doing bear defense firearms training for D.F.O., I have found these people to be very bear conservationist-minded. They experience much more bear danger hazard than any other type of field personnel, and bend over backwards to avoid killing bears.

Sometimes they have to make a quick clear decision for self preservation, as the following story will indicate:

Circumstances involving fisheries officer G.A. Rahier & Capt. J. Roche and the grizzly bear encounter/shooting that occurred August 14, 1991 on Johnston Creek Rivers Inlet, D.F.O. subdistrict.

Background: Johnston Creek is located about one-third of the way up Rivers Inlet on the east side and is one of the area's best pink salmon producers. The creek is comprised of three separate reaches: The first three-quarters of a mile is a fairly steep gradient, is comprised mainly of boulders, and is not generally used for spawning but a migration corridor; the second reach is about one mile long, and is a slow-moving pool that the pinks use to hold in prior to moving into the third reach, which has a low gradient and is ideal for spawning. Bears are mainly sighted on the first and third reaches as the shallow water allows them easy access to the fish. The year 1991 was an off-year for pinks, so escapements were projected to be low. It is a well-known fact that there is a high density of grizzly bears that frequent this drainage especially in years of high pink abundance. In 1989, a sow with twin two-year-old cubs was reported to be utilizing the estuary flats at low tide to forage for clams and cockels and would charge tourists in boats that would approach to take photographs. This family group was not sighted in 1989 or 1990 but D.F.O. staff that walked this system were made aware of their presence.

At approximately 13:15, Rahier/Roche were let off at the bottom of the creek with a canoe to be pulled up the first section of creek and left at the "Canoe Pool" to be used for enumeration throughout the season. Only two pinks were spotted in the first section of stream, and a handful of jumpers and finners in the lower end of the Canoe Pool.

They continued up the system in the canoe to see if pinks were present throughout the Canoe Pool. The wind was blowing upstream at five-to-ten mph and it was a clear, sunny day. At approximately 14:15 they were paddling through a narrow section about three-quarters of the way up the pool when a loud growling/roaring sound was heard in a dense clump of bush right on the stream bank. Rahier banged the paddle on the side of the canoe and both men yelled, but the bear was advancing quickly towards the edge of the stream. Rahier picked up his shotgun (four Federal 2-3/4" slugs up the tube - Remington 870), and racked a round. By this time the bear came into view on the bank 25 feet from the canoe and was still advancing when Rahier fired the first shot, and followed with a second round.

The bear was out of sight in the dense bush, and heavy labored breathing could be heard accompanied by gurgling sounds. The two backed off downstream to try to gain their composure. From the first sound heard, till the two shots were fired, only four to six seconds had expired.

After a couple minutes, they landed the canoe on the shore across from where the bear was sighted. Roche fired a round of #4 shot into the bush in an attempt to get the bear to move.

They stayed there for 35-40 minutes listening for any sounds that would indicate a wounded bear. There was the odd rustling, but the wind in the trees made it difficult to determine if its source was the bear. It was decided that they would have to cross the river and confirm the kill, or finish the bear off for the safety of future staff enumerating the system. The area around the clump of trees the bear was in was comprised of three to four foot tall grass.

The clump of bush was about 40 yards long and 30 yards wide, and was extremely dense. The two circled the entire clump about 25 yards out into the open field to allow visibility if they were charged again. They circled the outside of the clump of trees with no incident or sounds heard. The entire area surrounding the clump of trees was heavily utilized by bear. It was decided to enter from the downstream side, as it allowed the best visibility penetration into the bush, but still only six to ten feet visibility at best. About half-way through the clump a low whining noise was heard, and a slight bit of rustling. They continued to advance slowly. Roche sighted movement ahead and fired a slug. Then Roche, on his hands and knees, could see a yearling cub about ten feet away. Rahier instructed him to destroy the animal as they still hadn't spotted the sow and he was worried about having more than one bear to deal with at a time. Roche fired and killed the cub with one shot. This is the first time they were aware of any cubs present. Roche got down on his knees and continued looking. He spotted a second cub that was already dead only five feet in front of him. They advanced a few more feet and the sow was spotted dead, with the first cub sighted, dead beside her. With the thickness of the bush and the shade, visibility was very limited. Rahier shot the sow again between the shoulder blades to ensure she was dead. The second dead cub was probably the result of the second or fourth shots fired. From the time they crossed the river till all three bears were confirmed dead took about 40 minutes. The head and front paws were removed from the sow so the Conservation Officer Service could do measurements and determine age, weight and health of the bear. All three carcasses were rolled into the deep part of the river right below where the bodies were found so that other bears wouldn't scavenge the carcasses and possibly attack future staff working on the creek. The sow was estimated to be six to seven feet in length and weighed approximately 500 to 600 pounds. The cubs were this year's offspring.

G.A. Rahier, Fishery Officer
J.M. Roche, Capt. FPV Robson Reef

Author's note: When Greg (G.A. Rahier) saw that
the sow was about to launch herself into the canoe, he
knocked her over backwards with a shotgun slug to
the chest. He had taken my firearms training
course about three weeks prior to this attack, and
scored very high in weapon proficiency. He stated
shortly after the incident that he may not have been
at a level of awareness or reactionary capability to
have successfully concluded his defense, if he had
not just taken my bear hazard safety firearms
training.

* * *

The following is another Department of Fisheries
bear incident. The meticulous detail and quality of
this report reflects the personality of the author, Dave
Flegel.
Dave and I worked together to develop the mid coast
bear hazard map. He has tremendous knowledge
about coastal fish and wildlife. Dave has a keen
interest in conservation of grizzly bears; he also has
a keen interest in not being injured or killed by a
bear:

Summary of circumstances regarding a
grizzly bear encounter in the Kimsquit River,
B.C., August 27, 1990

Personnel Involved:
Stan Hutchings, Fishery Warden
Department of Fisheries and Oceans

Kevin McKenney, Contractor
Prov. Fish & Wildlife

David Flegel, Fishery Officer
Department of Fisheries and Oceans

Louis Malo, Master FPV
"Temple Rock"
Department of Fisheries and Oceans

On August 27, 1990, the aforementioned personnel were working on the Kimsquit River primarily to enumerate spawning chum salmon, and deal with some habitat protection responsibilities. Stan and Kevin had been working the river all day by river boat and on foot. The last channel of the day which needed counting was one known as "The Snake" by D.F.O. personnel. This slough is a meandering side channel of the Kimsquit River of approximately 4 km in length. It is located roughly about 1 km east of the Doman's logging camp on the west side of the Kimsquit River. The vegetation can best be described as dense underbrush consisting of elderberry, devil's club, salmon-berry, and stinging nettle overstoried by large mature cottonwood and spruce. No D.F.O. trails exist; a short one was made in 1989 but due to continual side channel change it was largely washed out. Travel is best done walking in the water, or on bear trails. The side channel averages 20 feet in width and generally has well defined banks of 2-4 feet.

At approximately 16:00 hours, Stan and Kevin tied the river boat off at the mouth of the side channel and proceeded to walk the slough. Stan had not been carrying a shotgun all day, as Kevin had been carrying his. Kevin was using a Model 1100 Remington Semi-Auto, loaded with shotgun slugs. When they left the boat Stan said, "I'll take my shotgun along. I always carry a gun on this stretch of water, and there should be two shotguns." Stan was walking ahead of Kevin most of the way, using the channel as a path and sometimes walking in the bush. Stan was 20-30 feet ahead of Kevin all the way. Stan was counting live chums, and Kevin was counting chum carcasses, and also looking for bear sign. (Kevin was on this trip to see how D.F.O. walked creeks and how we recorded grizzly bear sightings, as the Bella Coola Fishery Officers had started a grizzly sightings recording program the previous year which the Fish and Wildlife was interested in.)

Kevin explained, "We had been walking upstream for about 15 minutes. We reached a stretch of creek where the banks were about five feet vertical on either side, the creek was 15-20 feet wide - it had a slight meander. A point was reached when I heard a deep growl (Stan was still 20-30 feet ahead), the noise was 50 feet (measured later) behind me. I turned around to the noise, at the same instant a grizzly launched out of a deep hole in the bank 50 feet downstream from me." At this point Stan was still unaware of anything taking place.

Kevin continued, "There was deadfall in front of the hole - the grizzly took a leap out of the hole and cleared this deadfall, landing in six inches of water, its head was down at almost ground level, ears flatly laid back, mouth wide open - roaring all the time." Kevin watched this for an instant then thought, "This could be a bluff, but when the bear reached another deadfall ten feet away, I knew he meant business. I went to cock the mechanism on the shotgun, but I realized that at this point it was already too late, I had made my decision too late. The shotgun didn't cock all the way and I knew I wouldn't get it to my shoulder in time.

At this point I screamed, I was mad at myself for not having done something sooner, and at the same time I realized I was in Stan's line of fire.   I started to step backwards while I continued to try and free the action on the shotgun." At the same time, Stan had heard the growling and Kevin's scream.   Stan was carrying a Remington model 870 Wingmaster shotgun. It was in his right hand, with no shell in the chamber, breech unlocked, safety off, and four slugs in the magazine.

Stan explained, "I started an automatic turn, as I pumped the shotgun to load it when I heard the sounds. As I turned I brought the gun up to my shoulder and aimed.   The grizzly had changed course about two feet towards the right, it was now over the last log between where it had left the hole and Kevin. I aimed at the left shoulder and fired, it was just an instinctive shot."

At this point it was later measured that Kevin was standing eight feet out of the line of Stan's fire to Stan's right. When Stan fired the first shot the bear was 12 feet away from Kevin. When the shot went off the grizzly appeared to react and veered off to the right. Stan was standing 30 feet from the bear on the first shot.

Stan had a split second to make a decision, but said, "I judged that my first shot had hit the bear and had to shoot again, so I had reloaded and fired broad side at the bear" (now only 22 feet from Stan).

The bear kept going at 90 degrees from the creek, up the bank, and into the brush toward the east. These two shots fired were heard by Louis and David, and were so close together they thought it was a Semi-automatic being fired.

Stan went to reload after the second shot, but the spent shotshell casing from the second shot did not eject and jammed the gun (possibly short stroked the action).

After the bear went into the bush, Kevin heard it head east for about 50 metres and then turn south downstream. They listened for a moment to make sure there were no further sounds coming from the bear, then thought about the possibility of cubs in the area, so they checked the hole. No other grizzlies were seen. They spent some time looking in the area of the shooting, and where the grizzly went into the bush, but could find no sign of blood. Stan and Kevin spent more time looking at the hole the bear was in, and realized they had walked by the bear very closely without realizing it was there (later measured at 18 feet). They returned to the *Temple Rock* without incident.

At the *Temple Rock* it was decided that it would be too dangerous to return that evening to look for the bear, so it was left until the morning. The Provincial Conservation Officer was notified of the incident and what action was planned.

The following are other observations made by Stan and Kevin later in the evening when the details of this incident were recorded:

Kevin and Stan described the bear as medium size 250-275 lbs and chocolate brown in colour. Kevin had been assisting with tranquilizing and radio collaring grizzlies earlier in the week, and felt this bear was similar in size to some they had handled.

They had noted two sets of adult grizzly bear tracks downstream; one of the sets measured seven inches across the front paw. There were also cub prints around.

Up to the point of the bear encounter, 119 dead chums were observed, and 1,100 live chums. (Author's note: This is a good escapement of chums to this particular side channel.) Some pink salmon were also spawning in the channel.

The side channel was very noisy, with water running over logs and small riffles as well as the continual splashing of spawning salmon.

The wind was nearly negligible, either non-existent or perhaps a barely detectable outflow (from the north). It had been a very warm day, with quite a bit of cloud cover.

Stan commented that, "Had I been alone, I probably would not have heard the bear coming until it was too late" and, "had Kevin not been aware of the seriousness of the situation and not moved aside, he would have been in direct line between myself and the bear."

This was the first grizzly bear in 13 years of creek walking in grizzly bear country that Stan had to fire at with the intent to kill. In the previous 14 years Fishery Officers working on the Kimsquit have not had a serious bear incident requiring shooting a grizzly. In 1989 the Fishery Officers recorded 37 grizzly bear sightings on the Kimsquit River. This grizzly was the 24th sighting in that year. Stan and Kevin estimated that the whole encounter lasted four, possibly five, seconds.

At 07:15 hrs on August 28, 1990, the four same men returned to "The Snake" to attempt to determine the outcome of the shooting. We were all armed with shotguns. When we neared the site of the hole in the bank, three of us waited in the creek where we had good visibility of the channel and the hole, while Stan went up the bank into the bush across the

channel from the hole, to determine if the bear
was in the hole again. He started to throw rocks
into the hole, and then a grizzly bear stood up in
the bush on the far edge of the bank roughly
adjacent to where Stan had stood the previous
day when he fired at the bear. The grizzly was
identified by Kevin as being, as what he felt,
was the same bear that had charged them. Stan
was unable to see the bear from where he was at.
The bear showed no sign of aggression and
quickly moved off into the bush. We spent the
next 10-15 minutes watching to ensure the bear
did not come back and measuring the above
noted distances. Once we had recreated the
position of Stan, Kevin, and the bear, we began
searching for signs of the shots. At a point in
line with Stan's first shot and the bear, we
found a shotshell wad. In a small alder laying
behind where the bear was we found a fresh
gouge in the log, in the same line as the line of
fire. Although the gouge was not a direct hit it
definitely appeared to be part of a ricochet or
fragment. We assumed the first shot was a
total miss or perhaps a possible grazing of the
bear, or the shot hit the shallow water and rocks
and ricocheted up to the log. In the line of fire
for the second shot we found the shotshell wad
and a large direct hit of a slug into the log on the
bank behind - a definite clear miss.

Kevin crawled into the grizzly hole, while
Stan went downstream about 50 feet and shouted
in a similar manner to what noise would normally be made while creek walking. Kevin
could not hear any sounds, due to the effect of
the hole and a riffle of running water in front
of the hole.

We then started to look for signs of blood where
the bear entered the bush after it was shot and
we also looked a few feet upstream where we

had just seen the grizzly - no blood was found. When we left the area, we attempted to follow the freshly disturbed bush on the route that Stan and Kevin suspected the grizzly followed, but again no sign of blood. The four of us were convinced by sighting a grizzly which appeared to be the same bear back at the site, that the bear had not been injured.

The details of this incident were documented on the evening of the 27th of August, and the morning of the 28th, all distances were measured to verify the close proximity of the grizzly.

Recorded by: David Flegel, Fishery Officer, Bella Coola, B.C.

Author's note: The most important event in the preceding story is that the first shot turned the bear away. The shotgun slug probably splashed the bear with gravel and water.

Shortly after this incident the local D.F.O. office in Bella Coola hired me to investigate this incident, and to also spend a day doing fish enumeration with Lyle Enderud and Dave Flegel.

I submitted the following report to the Bella Coola D.F.O. office.

Sept. 11, 1990
Lyle Enderud
Fisheries Officer
D.F.O.
Bella Coola, B.C.

Re: Bear Hazard assessment of lower Kimsquit River and examination of fish enumeration methodology.

Dear Lyle;

I enjoyed the field trip of the 9th and 10th. You have a good crew working for you. Before I make comments about what I saw on our trip I would like to give you some background about my past experience and present knowledge.

When I moved to Bella Coola in 1965 my main hobby was bear hunting. After a few years, I became interested in bears from a biological point of view and have studied them ever since. Right from the beginning, I specialized in taking large old males and limited myself to killing a grizzly every four or five years - this of course does not include problem or aggressive bears that I had to eliminate over the years. I always hunted spring and fall every year and spent a lot of my time watching sows with cubs, or young lone grizzlies going about their business. I spent hours studying bear trees and bear sign in order to make sense of their meanderings. I also started reading all of the published bear studies that I could get my hands on. Eventually I became not only interested but also involved in bear conservation.

Over the years I became aware of how difficult grizzlies could be to kill at times, and also aware of how many things can go wrong when a bear is breathing down your neck. I learned quickly that none of the factory rifle ammunition had well enough constructed bullets to plow through the shoulder and spinal bones of a large bear. I started with a 30-30, then a 30-06, then a .350 Remington Magnum, and now a .358 Norma Magnum. I have tested several thousand bullets in wood and wallboard mediums, examined about 35 wound channels in bears and collected the bullets, tested a whole range of weapons including handguns, and carefully analyzed what goes wrong with people and weapons when facing a dangerous bear. There is one simple fact: You have to kill a lot of bears in order to learn how to do it effectively.

In the last 25 years I've had approximately 50 close encounters with grizzly bears. Half of those bears ran away immediately, the other half displayed boldness or aggressive charges, and two came full tilt with the intention of killing me. In most cases I was hunting upwind and jumped bedded bears at ranges from three metres to 70 metres. Most of the aggressive encounters have been in the last 15 years and reflect changing bear behaviour.

From about 1975 on, there was a noticeable increase in bear attacks in the mid coast. I became interested in bear defense in about 1980 when I became aware of some of the problems that logging company engineers and Forestry employees were having. Between 1980 and 1987 I instructed quite a few individuals who came to me requesting bear defense information.

When the Ministry of Forests came out with its firearms training policy in 1987 the local district office approached me about giving a bear defense course. In 1988 I sat in on a course as an observer that was given to local Forestry employees by the Provincial police training officer. It was a good firearms course, but the bear part was minimal and the safety techniques were not as advanced as mine.

It took until 1989 to get the legalities and policies sorted out to a point that I could proceed with developing my own firearms training, as requested by the local forestry office. Presently I have ten Forestry and five Parks employees as participants. Two more people are to start this year. I have received good feedback regarding the course, and as far as I can tell, it's a success. One thing is for sure, there is no other course like it in Canada.

One important component of my course is bear avoidance. This aspect works well for forestry and parks personnel, but most fisheries employees break all the rules of bear avoidance. This means that more emphasis must be put on quick defense when warranted. Also, all practice would have to simulate the fish counting method - talleywackers tied off and in hand. Some of the existing course procedures are not appropriate to Fisheries personnel. The course would work well for full time employees but an altered crash course with follow-up may be necessary for part-time staff. But if they work for one year only, it will be wasted money.

I would like to give you my impressions of what I saw on our field trip. The first section of creeks, side sloughs, and river that we covered from Pollard Creek to the Snake Slough fit into one category, and the lower Snake Slough into another. The first area had numerous fresh tracks but a shortage of scats and beds. This indicates primarily nocturnal use with the bears probably crossing the river and bedding four or five hundred metres into the bush. This doesn't mean that you won't run into bears in the daytime, it means that statistically you run into less bears than in high-day-use areas. This area is too open and has too much road noise to meet most bears' bedding requirements.

When we got about half-way down the Snake, things changed. Scats became frequent and fresh beds were within ten metres of the bank in many places. This area meets most bears' requirements for day activity and bedding. I suspect though that most Kimsquit bears are at least slightly manwise and careful all the time. As people have known for some time, the Snake slough is a high hazard area that requires special precautions. When I examined the bear bed and area where the incident took place, I felt that the guys had been lucky as encounter situations don't get much worse than that and I don't see any way it could have been avoided. The bear had himself cornered and no matter how you would have approached him you would be on top of him before he sensed you. It just comes down to being able to defend yourself.

Things have evolved to the point, in some coastal drainages, that you are going to have to change your methods. In high hazard areas there should always be two people, and both *armed*. In a place like the "Snake" one person should be counting fish and the other watching for bears. The defender should be walking the top of the bank, where possible, and slightly ahead of the counter. From this position I could see at least twice as far and I would have been able to see a bear stand up from a bed on either side of the slough. A defender would have much more control over an encounter situation and because of his height neither person would be in the other's line of fire.

Wherever possible you should have upstream and downstream boat or road access so that you can travel down-wind. Most bears will vacate the area as soon as they smell human scent. Try to avoid high hazard areas after 5:00 p.m. as many bears become active soon after.

It appeared to me that six to eight mature bears and two cubs were active in the area that we walked. One large male, one smaller male, one sow with a first-year cub, one sow with a second-year cub, and three or four intermediate tracks. This is about the expected ratio for high population areas.

Respectfully, James Gary Shelton

* * *

Let's now take a side excursion back about 20 years to when I was at my peak in exploring grizzly behaviour. The following story is courtesy of the *Williams Lake Tribune*, dated July 1974:

Williams Lake man mauled by grizzly

A Williams Lake man was mauled by a grizzly while his 11-year-old daughter made her escape during a fishing trip on the Atnarko River near Bella Coola Saturday.

Recovering at home with a punctured shin bone and lacerations is Norm Kadoski of 1255 N. 11th Ave., a shovel operator at the Gibraltar Mine. His daughter, Carol, was unharmed.

The attack occurred while the two were walking back from a fishing spot on a narrow trail through thick brush.

Kadoski and his daughter had come to a turn in the trail where a small path runs down to the river when they encountered the grizzly on the main path.

Kadoski held the bear off with his fishing rod for a split second while his daughter fled down the small pathway to the river.

The grizzly chewed the rod down to about the handle, and Kadoski turned to run. The bear seized him by the leg. He broke away and found himself in the river with his daughter in waist-deep water. The bear remained on shore.

Their cries for help attracted the attention of a

fishing party nearby which came to investigate and scared the bear off.

Kadoski was carried to Bella Coola Hospital for treatment.

His family said Wednesday that the swelling on his leg was down, but that he would remain off the job for some time.

Author's note: I knew this five-year-old male grizzly well. I had dubbed him "Moe". He had previously been part of a family group I called "Meany, Miney, and Moe". His mother and sister had both been killed the year before in separate incidents. Moe was raised by the most dangerous and aggressive sow ("Meany") I had ever seen.

This sow was aggressive when she showed up on the Atnarko in late June of 1969 with Miney and Moe, who were cubs of the year. During June of the following year this family group developed "family defense behaviour". Instead of the cubs running away from a threat, they would join mom in aggressive displays towards an intruder. This group put the run on many a fisherman, and whenever I ran into them, I would back off quickly.

In the week before Moe attacked the Williams Lake man, I had had two run-ins with this bear. In both cases I was in a boat and he eventually stopped following and doing aggressive displays. On the evening after the attack I called Fisheries warden Bob Ratcliff to let him know how many spring salmon I had caught in the two previous days. Bob asked me if I had heard about the attack. I said "No", and he gave me the details; he then expressed the same concern about this dangerous bear that I had.

The next morning I was up at 4:30 a.m. and on my way; the drift boat was in the truck. I was in the river by 5:30 a.m. and started a long day of drifting for a ways, then beaching and walking grizzly high-use areas searching for Moe. By 6:00 p.m. I had given up for the day and felt a little disappointed.

The next morning I was on the river at about the same time and started the process again. At about 11:00 a.m. I walked up on a sow with a first-year cub who were both bedded under a large cedar. When this sow finally recognized what it was she was squinting at, they were off to the races. At that time there were only two grizzlies on the Atnarko who were not terrified of humans.

On the third day I took a break and got caught up on delayed work. That night I called Bob Ratcliff to see if there had been any sightings of Moe. He said, "No, not that I know of." The next morning I started again but decided to drift a longer section of river that included the upper Bella Coola. I also had a different plan. I would move along faster and check main river crossing spots for Moe's fresh 6 1/8" wide front pad track.

Each time I stopped it would take a little while to sort out the dozens of overlapping tracks. The larger sow tracks were about the same size as Moe's, but usually a paralleling set of cub or cub's tracks would give them away. I didn't get very far past the confluence onto the Bella Coola when I found the right size tracks - everywhere. Moe had been busy since the attack, but had shifted his activity area about six kilometres west.

I checked several spots and found his bed from two days before. At about 4:00 p.m. I stopped at one of my favorite spots where there was an old trapper's cabin in a small clearing. I pulled the boat up and tied it off, then climbed the bank and walked about 100 metres, just short of the cabin clearing, and stopped.

I stood looking at the cabin wondering about the people who had lived there 50 years earlier. My thoughts weren't even on bears when I heard the rattling of low hanging cedar limbs off to my right, near the river. I carefully, quietly, chambered a round into my 30-06, and waited. There was a slight westerly breeze blowing from where the noise had come from.

I saw the dark shape in the brush just before it came out into the clearing. It looked like Moe all right, but darker; he was soaking wet. He must have just crossed the river. He stood looking at the cabin for a minute then proceeded into the clearing. I was convinced it was Moe, and I knew I could confirm his identity by behaviour.

When he was right in front of me, 30 metres away, I yelled, "Hey Moe." He looked, then slowly turned to face me. I yelled again, "How's it going Moe?" Moe dropped his head and turned it slightly sideways as his ears flattened out. This was the first signal Moe used in his "I don't like people" repertoire.

I knew what was coming next, but I wasn't at all nervous. I had the front bead centered in the rear peep sight, and I was lined up on the spine just above the head. Moe would do a slow, growling, head-down approach. I decided that just in case Moe had a change-up in tactics, to fool me, I would tap the trigger with his first step.

The 180 grain Nosler severed Moe's spinal chord between the third and fourth vertebrae.

* * *

Ministry of Forests personnel and silvicultural contractors are particularly vulnerable to bear attacks. In some areas of the province they have worked for years occasionally running into bears that usually ran off quickly. But in the last few years these people are running into more bears, and some that do not run off.

Doug Gibbs told me that when he is spotting and marking beetle-infested trees he walks through the timber looking up at tree crowns for dead tops. Often he is not paying attention to what is going on at ground level. In the following story he did notice something out of the ordinary at ground level, but didn't recognize the danger he was in until it was too late:

I have been working for the Ministry of Forests for eight years. In the summer I work in the fire protection section. During the winter I work for the silvicultural department and do projects related to forest health.

On the day of my bear attack (November 24, 1993), my job was to assist our Mountain Pine Beetle contractor with the location of small beetle infestations, and to monitor the falling and burning of infested trees. The three members of the contract crew (Kevin, Brad, and Wayne) and I would be working the southeast slope of Vama Mountain at an elevation of about 900 metres.

We had been working since 9:00 a.m. and it appeared to be like any other day. While the crew ate lunch I went ahead and marked out the next work site. While ribboning the infested trees I noticed a large spruce blowdown that had broken off at the stump. The stump was still anchored to the ground in a normal position.

I noticed a hole going under the root system of the stump. There were about six inches of snow on the ground and there was limb debris under the snow where this 12 inch diameter opening went under the stump. It appeared to be something that an animal might use, but only a small animal could fit into the hole. There was no animal sign or disturbance in the two-week-old snow around the opening, nor was there any major dirt pile from digging. I placed a ribbon ten feet away from it so we wouldn't disturb the site in case a small animal was using it.

The crew caught up with me at about 12:50 p.m.

and the faller (Kevin) started working immediately. Brad was spotting for Kevin so Wayne
and I walked down to look at the hole under the
stump by the blowdown. We were on a steep,
snow-covered hill-side that made walking
awkward. We could still hear the saw working above us when we got to the hole. We stood
looking at it from a distance of about 15 feet.

Wayne seemed very nervous and all of a sudden he took off running back up the hill. (I
found out later that he saw the snow move by the
opening.) I had watched him start up the hill
and when I looked back at the hole I saw a bear
dart out of it and start lunging at me - the bear
was growling.

I turned so fast to run that my feet went out
from under me just as the bear was about to
make contact. The bear missed me, lost its
footing, then went rolling down the hill-side
and landed up against a fallen tree. We were
both up instantly; the bear stood up on its hind
legs and growled again. I could see it was a
large black bear.

The bear was after me again and my only
thought was to evade this thing. I headed across
the hill-side and instinctively started dodging
around some small immature trees in order to
slow the bear down. It was right behind me and
I was able to keep ahead of it for about 20
seconds.

Then I felt the awful pain as its teeth sank into
my upper thigh. I grabbed onto a small three
inch tree; the bear was trying to pull me to the
ground. All of my body muscles were being
pulled and stretched hard; I was trying to avoid
going down. The bear only tugged at my leg
for about five seconds, then let go, stepped to my
side, and knocked me down with a front paw. I
landed in a sitting position and all I could see

was these teeth coming at me. I put my arm up just as it bit for my face; the terrible pain was back.

The bear had sunk its canine teeth into my hand and was pulling so hard this time that I couldn't resist; I was going down. I felt that I had lost the struggle with the bear. All of a sudden it let go and ran off at top speed.

During the attack I was not aware of anything else going on. Wayne had run up the hill and got Kevin to run down the hill revving up his saw in order to chase the bear off. The bear pressed the attack until they were only 30 feet away. What seemed like forever probably lasted no more than a minute.

I wasn't bleeding too badly and I was able to walk back to the helicopter pad opening where we had been dropped off in the morning. The crew had radio-called for the chopper and I was at the Prince George Hospital within 40 minutes of the attack.

I was off work for a short period of time. I did not have any infection and the wounds have healed up nicely. But I hate to think about how different the outcome of this incident might have been if I had been working by myself.

Wayne told me later that when the armed crew went in the next day to insure that it was safe to resume work in the area, they discovered that the bear had dug a shallow den and had pulled limbs over itself for additional cover. The opening at ground level was somewhat larger than the opening in the snow that we had been looking at.

Before this happened I was not very well schooled about bears or their habits. I feel that your bear safety course has helped me considerably. From now on I intend to follow the encounter guidelines that you present in your training material.

Author's note: Doug attended one of my bear hazard safety courses in May of 1994. At the end of the day and just before I gave my encounter survival guidelines, I asked him whether he thought "playing dead or fighting back" would have been appropriate with his bear attack. He said he didn't have a clue, and there was no time for such decisions anyway.

In my opinion this bear was acting defensive-aggressive in relation to its den, but very likely would have turned predatory once it got Doug down on the ground.

If it was a large male black bear, as Doug thought, it probably would have tried a killing bite to the throat as soon as it had the opportunity.

* * *

I have heard quite a few stories in the last three years pertaining to Forestry personnel or loggers having den site encounters with black bears. Most of these bears are lethargic and slowly move off, but some are aggressive.

I know a young faller by the name of Richard Ratcliff; he told me the following story:

I was falling a four-foot-diameter hemlock tree on a steep hill-side setting in Nusatsum Valley (a side valley to Bella Coola Valley) on April 2, 1992. After I made the undercut I could see that the tree was completely hollow and supported by a narrow outer ring of wood. I put my hand into the undercut and cleaned out some debris. Then I put the backcut in and watched the tree go over.

When the tree hit the ground it rolled down the hill-side about 40 feet. I started to run down to it - to buck it - when I saw a black bear come out of the butt. When it got its bearings it started up the hill in a very nasty mood; I nervously started back up the hill. I kept the saw running and when I passed the stump two tiny bawling cubs were trying to climb out of it.

When I got about 50 yards up the hill I stopped and watched a very angry mother bear try to console her cubs. I moved to another area to work in order to give her some time to remove her cubs to a safe spot. But, two days later the bears were still in the area of the stump. We amended the falling boundary and left them alone.

There wasn't an entry hole into the den at the bottom of the tree. I never got back to the tree to buck it, but the tree had a kink about 12 feet up and there was probably a hole at that spot.

The sow must have climbed up inside as I cut up the tree, as my cut level was just above the top of the nest.

* * *

The following report was supplied to me by Myron Zukewich, who is Jim Hart's able assistant in the Fort Nelson Conservation Officer Service:

This report concerns the mauling of one Ava Watkins (approximately 70 years) of Anchorage, Alaska by a black bear boar approximately two years old.

On May 16th, 1992, around 14:00, Ava Watkins was north bound on the Alaska Highway with her husband Truman, and her companion Lahoma Cook. At km 770, Prochniak Creek, and still within the Muncho Lake Park area, they spotted a black bear that was feeding on the road. A truck with a box-camper was already at this location and the occupants of the vehicle appeared to be photographing the bear.

Lahoma Cook, of California, had taken several opportunities to photograph wildlife on the trip and as the bear presented an inviting subject they pulled over. From the vehicle window, Lahoma photographed the bear and Ava elected to exit the vehicle to get a closer photograph. The vehicle at this time was positioned on the west side of the road and the bear was at the edge of the ditch against the timber on the extreme east of the highway. No other vehicles were in the area.

Ava took her photograph on the highway and turned to return to the van in which she was travelling. The bear, at this time, was moving towards her but she was not aware of the intentions of the bear. Assuming that it was a "docile, harmless bear," she did not hurry or hear the shouts from her companions to hurry into the van. They, from their seats in the vehicle, watched the bear quicken his pace towards Ava, who was slowly returning to the van. At the point where she opened the door to step up to enter the van, the bear was upon her. He approached the final three feet on his hind legs and bit tightly onto her left shoulder, not letting go. Dropping back down on four legs, the bear then dragged her off her feet, backwards and head-first towards the woods. At this location the bear continued his assault to the left shoulder, then moved to the right shoulder and then to the left arm. The other travellers, also elderly, offered assistance by throwing objects such as rocks and sticks at the bear. They had little effect other than to stop the biting on Ava, however, the bear would not leave her side. Some of these rocks, the bear investigated by chasing them where they landed. It is possible that the bear had been fed by previous tourists and expected that the rocks were offerings thrown to it.

Truman Watkins required crutches and as such, could only watch as his wife was being chewed upon by the black bear. Lahoma at this time left the vehicle and took with her Truman's crutch. Approaching the bear, she connected once on the snout of the bear causing minor bruising to that area. The bear, according to Truman, was little concerned with Lahoma but her attack with the crutch caused him to yet again relent on his attack on Ava. Ava moved at one point and the bear ran back and continued to chew on her shoulders which was met with more screams and rocks thrown by the bystanders. For a brief moment, the black bear actually left Ava and returned to the road, standing between the vehicles that were parked. The driver of the other vehicle yelled to Truman to drive over the bear. In the time taken to start the motor, the bear had returned to Ava and stood over her again. Here he took Ava's head into his mouth, did not clamp down, but left slight wounds. Letting go, the bear watched the road and paced while the onlookers threw rocks and yelled at it. Lahoma continued to defend Ava with the crutch when she could. Finally, after about ten minutes, a group of vehicles stopped to assist. A semi-truck driver also stopped and found a very large tree limb that he was prepared to attack the bear with. First, he placed Lahoma back into the safety of the van. Then he began throwing large rocks at the bear with the assistance of another unknown male. According to Truman and Lahoma, a particularly large rock landed very close to the bear and the bear backed off and entered the bush. At this time, both men rushed to Ava and as she lay still, each grabbed an ankle and pulled her straight back from the edge of the bush. Truman stated that the presence of the adult males had a distinct effect in discouraging the bear from his attack as opposed to the bear's unconcerned reactions to Lahoma and others throwing rocks at the bear. Ava was then helped to her feet and she began walking back to the van. The bear again came out of the bush and began pacing and watching the scene. Everyone evacuated the area with Ava enroute to a hospital. The episode lasted about 15 to 20 minutes. This bear showed very distinct signs of a predacious attack and was not about to leave his prey. No vocalizations were heard from the bear and it seemed to be wary of people but showed little fear.

South-bound, the Watkins alerted the Lodge to assist with an ambulance and told the story of the attack. Ava did not go into shock and remained talking during her ride into Fort Nelson General Hospital.

The RCMP in Fort Nelson were alerted and they responded to the scene assuming the bear was still at large. The Conservation Officer in the area also responded to the mauling after checking with a bear hunter who had advised him that a mauling had occurred at Muncho Lake. Both vehicles responded Code 3.

Park rangers in the area of Liard were advised that a bear was "causing a problem on the highway" but were not advised of the mauling. Cam Hill attended the scene to see a bear with a bruise upon his nose. The bear approached Hill, who was seated in his truck, and the bear placed his nose up to the open window. This was received by a blast from the canister of bear repellent that Hill had on his person. The bear, very obviously affected by this, immediately retreated into the woods swatting his nose and head area. Hill contemplated destroying the bear but let the repellent send a message to the bear instead. Obviously, had he been aware the bear had moments before mauled a tourist, it would have been destroyed at this time.

The other tourists at the mauling scene headed north and told the episode to Lower Liard Lodge proprietor Gene Bietz. Bietz immediately took his firearm and attended the scene to find the bear yet at the scene with other tourists stopping to observe the bear. He quickly advised them of the previous tourist's misfortune and dispatched the bear. It had the markings on its snout from the blows Lahoma laid upon it with the crutch. Park Ranger Al Hansen, finding out about the attack, also attended moments behind Bietz to observe the bear's carcass. The bear was sexed to be a male and was in poor shape. Little else is known about the bear as it was taken to the Liard River and dumped into the flowing water.

The bear's demise was relayed to the RCMP and the Conservation Officer and RCMP broke off their response and attended at regular patrol speeds.

Ava Watkins was transferred twice by ambulances that set out from Toad River and Fort Nelson. The van met the first ambulance that set out south-bound and delivered Ava to a second ambulance which ultimately ended up in Fort Nelson General Hospital. There she was treated for over 40 puncture wounds and given 100 plus stitches. More stitches would be required to close the tears and lacerations to her shoulders, however, there was risk of infection and the wounds were bandaged to allow for drainage with regular changing of the dressing. Both Ava and Truman have been around bears for over 40 years and they did not consider the bear dangerous. They stated that they realized how very lucky they were and that they should have known better. Ava held no harsh feelings toward the "wilderness" after her encounter and felt the bear was doing what came naturally to him in his territory.

Author's note: There seems to be two types of black bear attacks going on in Northern B.C. The first type involves wild bears with no human experience; the second type involves bears who are in the first-phase of human-food-habituation. The second category of bears are quite often third-year males.

When I analyze information from black bear studies that are done in the eastern U.S., then compare that information to what I know about black bears in northern B.C., it seems to be two different species. They are of course the same species, but their aggressive natures are totally different.

Black bears down south have several hundred years of learned behaviour about fearing people that is transmitted from mother to offspring. But there might be more to it. In most southern areas, bears have access to mast (oak acorns, beech nuts, etc.). This type of food is high in fat content. I'm suspicious that black bears in the far northern ecosystems are fat-starved for at least the first half of the year. Bears in these areas are very predatory towards moose calves, cariboo calves, small mammals, and occasionally towards people. There is also no large contingent of farmers and ranchers endlessly killing off predatory type bears.

* * *

The following is another roadside incident that happened August 22, 1993 and is courtesy of *The Province* newspaper:

Bear shot after mauling tourist
By Stuart Hunter, Staff Reporter

Tourist Nadia Aleix just wanted a snapshot of
a black bear but ended up getting an extreme
close-up of the burly bruin's temper.

Aleix, 30, of Andorra, a small country between
Spain and France, suffered serious leg
injuries when she was attacked by the bear
Thursday afternoon.

Clearwater RCMP Cpl. Doug Hindle said
Aleix and Albert Verges, also of Andorra,
pulled off Yellowhead Highway about 25 kilometres north of Blue River and followed the
camera-shy bear into the bush.

"I guess the bear didn't want its picture taken,
so it charged Aleix and grabbed her," Cpl.
Hindle said. "Verges threw rocks at the bear
until it let go."

But the two-year-old bear charged the pair
again as they scrambled to their vehicle. It
chased Aleix around the car until it caught her
and began gnawing on her leg.

Passing trucker Mike Parker, of Penhold,
Alberta, pulled over and saved Aleix by beating
the 52 kilogram bear over the head with a tire
iron.

Aleix was taken to Kamloops Royal Inland
Hospital, where she underwent surgery on her
legs.

The bear was shot dead by a passing motorist
about an hour after the mauling.

"The sad part, from the animal's side, is it
was only doing what nature told it to do,"
Hindle said.

Author's note: Many American and European tourist that come to B.C. assume that our roadside black

bears are tame, like the ones in Yellowstone or Yosemite Parks.

Most of these bears are wild or just slightly habituated to cars and people. They are usually at the roadside because of the grass that has been seeded on the shoulder. Some of these bears are very dangerous.

The most interesting aspect about the above incident was the outrage expressed by some individuals and groups about the bear being killed. These people claimed that the tourist did a stupid thing and the bear was acting "naturally".

I want to make an important statement here: Many types of bear attacks are of a nature that the bear involved will probably never again be dangerous to another person. But this attack has all the earmarks of a predatory attack. If this bear had not been killed, it might well have ended up on the outskirts of a town shortly after and attacked someone else. It could have even ended up in the yard of one of the individuals who were so outraged by the bear's death.

If predatory behaviour is involved in an attack, it doesn't matter whether a person has done something foolish or not, the bear must be destroyed because the bear will most likely be predatory towards someone else in the future who hasn't made a foolish mistake.

* * *

The *Cranbrook Daily Townsman* in Cranbrook, B.C. was nice enough to let me use this story:

Spray wards off charging bear
May 1993, by Carol Johner

Simon Davidson of St. Mary's Lake Road is used to the back country and he's used to wildlife.

What he's not used to is being charged by a fully-grown adult grizzly and it was only quick thinking on his part, and advice from his mother that kept the 20-year-old alive - with all his limbs intact.

Friday afternoon, Davidson was working in the bush in the Elk Valley, when he heard the sounds of an animal moving about. Familiar with the back country he didn't pay much attention, thinking perhaps it was an elk.

When he heard the sounds again, much closer this time, Davidson became concerned and reached into his backpack for a can of bear repellent spray - spray his mother suggested he pack just before he left.

About five seconds later, Davidson looked up and saw a grizzly rear up and charge directly toward him, crashing through the thick Lodgepole pine. No time to think, Davidson raised his can of bear spray, pointed and shot.

He saw the bear grab its eyes with its paws, and veer off to the side. Davidson continued to spray, following the bear's head.

Realizing he had stopped the bear's charge for the time being, Davidson started running back to his vehicle, which was a good one-half hour away.

"I was frightened for sure. It happened so fast. If that spray didn't save my life, it certainly saved my limbs and scalp and a lot of pain and suffering," said Davidson.

Davidson, who had never encountered a bear before, didn't want to make a lot out of the incident, saying people encounter bears all the time.

But a hiker who had heard about it reported it, saying people ought to know that bear spray, the cayenne pepper-based variety, works.

Simon's father Neil is of the same mind,

saying although his family had a can of the spray, they had never had to use it and therefore weren't sure of its effectiveness.

"I'm grateful for the development of this spray. I've had to shoot a bear before and I had to use three rounds from a .308 rifle, and the bear still travelled a good 300 metres," he said, adding he'd far rather have something that wouldn't hurt the bear long-term.

Neil said his family now has two cans of the spray, which is available at some local outlets, and they plan to take it whenever they travel into the wilderness.

Author's note: Even though pepper spray does not always work against bears, there are many people saving themselves from death or injury each year in North America by using it for defense against bears.

* * *

I received this report recently from Jim Hart. Let me introduce you to the players. First we have a black bear that is at some level of human-garbage-habituation. Next we have Myles Thorp who has been taking my bear hazard safety training for the last two years. Myles was driving along the Alaskan Highway and noticed a man lying under a vehicle, and very close to a bear trying to get into a garbage can. Myles knows about predacious black bear behaviour. He also knows that a person lying on the ground is much more vulnerable to attack.

Our third player is Al Hansen. Al has also been taking my training in recent years and he is an absolute expert at gun handling and safety. He is like many of our excellent B.C. Parks employees: He won't kill a bear unless he is convinced it's necessary.

Finally Al is convinced that Myles is right and

does what he must. Pay particular attention to how the bear responds to the spray:

Subject: Bear incident South of Stone Mountain Park

On July 16, 1993, at the litter pull-out one quarter mile north of Tetsa River Bridge #1 on the Alaskan Highway, I noticed a black bear attempting to gain entry to the garbage containers; two vehicles were parked nearby in front of the garbage bin. One man was on the ground half way under his vehicle attempting mechanical repairs. Another man, from the second vehicle, appeared to be standing guard as he was carrying a can of "Counter Assault" bear spray and had a rifle on the seat of his vehicle. After talking with him I learned his name was Myles Thorp and he works with the B.C. Forest Service in Fort Nelson. He related to me that he had driven by two hours earlier, saw the bear at the garbage bin and also the broken-down vehicle with the owner underneath who was trying to fix it. Myles felt obliged to pull his vehicle between the bear and the other vehicle and to stand guard in case the bear got frustrated with the garbage bin and decided to check out the tourist lying on the ground as several attempts to scare the bear away had failed. Locals at Summit Lodge had told Myles earlier that a black bear had been seen at the litter pull-out each of the two days prior to this for the better part of each day.

Myles told me that just prior to my arrival he was ready to shoot the bear and urged me to do it instead. As it was out of the Park, I thought I would try to scare it away, so I approached the bear using the garbage container for cover, moved around the end of the container and gave the bear a three-second blast of "Counter Assault" bear spray full in the face at a distance of four feet. The bear spun around and ran over a bank to the river in thick bush. Within three minutes the bear came back up over the bank and approached Myles and me. I moved towards the bear and he kept coming closer as well, until, at a distance of six feet I gave him another 1 1/2-second blast of spray in the face. He ran into the thick brush beside the garbage bin, but we could still see him moving around.

At this point the tourist fixed his vehicle and left. Myles left as well after urging me to shoot the bear for public safety. At this point another tourist pulled up to the garbage bin to deposit litter. The bear came back out of the bush and approached the garbage bin.

Ardith Thompson, Park Facility Operator, who was with me at the time, advised the tourist to try another pull-out. From the garbage laying around the bin I surmise this had happened several times in the last two days, people dropping their garbage on the ground as the bear came out of the bush or from behind the bin.

I approached the bear again. It wouldn't leave the area around the bin, but would circle around trying to keep some distance between us. Finally it stopped and faced me. I approached to within eight feet and gave it a one -second blast of spray. This time I pursued the bear into the bush, but it circled back towards the litter container where I gave it another one-second blast. At this point it was wary of me and would run a short distance when I sprayed, so I don't know how much spray actually made contact.

I then decided to pursue the bear and throw rocks at him. I managed to hit him a couple of times and he would run a short distance, circle, and come back behind us near the garbage corral. After a half-hour of this, I decided the bear wouldn't leave, and as other vehicles were pulling in continually, and being warned off by Ardith, I waited until the traffic cleared and shot the bear. Ironically, there wasn't even any garbage in the containers or any strong smell from them.

Both Fort Nelson Conservation Officers (C.O.s) were out of town at the time but I notified them of the incident upon their return and they supported the way in which I dealt with the potentially dangerous situation.

Al Hansen, Park Ranger

Author's note: The C.O.s and Parks employees that patrol the Alaskan Highway north of Fort Nelson have a difficult job because tourists feed bears at roadside pullouts. Guess what? B.C. does not have a law prohibiting people from feeding bears outside of parks. There should be a law, with fines ranging from $2,000 to $5,000, and strict enforcement. Almost every bear that is fed will either injure someone or will have to be killed. This is especially true in the northern part of the province.

Now that I have said that, I want to reiterate a key point of this book: Only about a third of injuries and deaths caused by bears in B.C. (outside of parks) are related to habituated bears or people doing something wrong with bears.

There are many people who try to blame the victim of a bear attack for causing the incident. These people are afraid that if bears get too much bad publicity the general public will be less interested in protecting them.

If you carefully examine the Alaskan bear attack data for the last ten years you will find that the majority of attacks are by coastal grizzlies (brown bears) and grizzlies in Denali Park, and are usually the result of sudden close-range encounters. There are, of course, Alaskan attacks that do fall into the spoiled-bear or people-mistake category. Alaska has always had a high percentage of attacks that are inflicted on people who are hunting coastal deer or grizzly bear. But even the majority of these are the result of sudden encounters. Some attacks are the result of wounded bears going after the hunter.

In a 1993 medical review of eight bear-inflicted deaths in Alberta between 1973 and 1988, it was determined that at least five of the eight bears involved had little or no prior human contact. Half of the eight were black bears, the other half grizzlies.

Here on the coast of B.C., black bear attacks are uncommon. Most bear attacks here are the result of close-range encounters with grizzlies, similar to the Alaskan data. When you look at the bear encounter data for B.C. (not attack data), it becomes obvious that most encounters are simply the result of people and bears accidentally getting too close to each other, or the result of predatory interest by a bear.

To my knowledge, I am the only person in B.C. who is collecting bear encounter data. This type of information is always undervalued for its importance and usually rejected by government agencies and most biologists. If there was a set of statistics that showed how many North Americans have successfully defended themselves against bears with firearms in the last ten years, a very different picture would emerge about bear aggressive behaviour.

* * *

In the *Bear Aggressive Behaviour* chapter I presented information about types of bear aggression. I explained that the main components of these behavioural traits have to do with social-regulatory population control mechanisms. I am convinced that in high quality habitats there is very little nutritional regulation taking place in bear populations, especially with grizzly bears.

When a grizzly population reaches near maximum level in a place like Bella Coola Valley, a significant portion of the cubs and sub-adults are killed each year by dominant-breeding-males. The "natural regimists" are people who believe in a wonderful balanced nature where animals can do no wrong and people do not belong. They claim that any event in nature is okay, as long as man is not involved. Carefully consider the following event that I witnessed in October of 1972. Decide for yourself whether it is better to let nature use social-regulatory-cub-killing-behaviour to limit bear populations, or to use selective hunting (that primarily targets large males) for reducing bear populations below the critical-regulatory-stress level:

This was the fourth hike I had made into the Talchako River Valley to hunt grizzly bears. I was by myself, and it took 8 1/2 hours to get to the third cabin (30 kilometres) at the Gyllenspetz Creek. On the way in I had checked the condition of the raft that Darryl Hodson and I had air-dropped and hung it in a tree. I had picked a spot for the drop that would put me below the bad section of log jams and sweepers that choked the river about five kilometres below the cabin. The last half hour of the day I had travelled in the dark, not very much fun considering the amount of grizzly sign.

The cabin I was going to stay in was built in 1936 by Bob Ratcliff and Albert White. Albert told me that he had never been so happy as when they got the fourth round of logs up and could move in for sleeping. They had been camping

on the river bar, and even though they were seasoned veterans of the bush, they were kept
awake each night by endless noises.

I had stayed in this cabin several times and
was glad that the original builders were tall
men; the bed was about seven feet long and still
in good repair. But the roof was a disaster, so I
had packed in a shake frow, and a file for
sharpening the old six-foot crosscut saw,
known as a "misery whip".

I spent the first day cutting rounds off a fallen
cedar, splitting shakes, ripping old shakes off,
then nailing new shakes on. Every couple of
hours, I would take my rifle and walk down to
the point across from the Gyllenspetz and sit for
a while. I didn't really expect to see anything
because of my work noise, but I just had to do a
little hunting that first day.

The next morning I was up two hours too early,
and excited about the day to come. I got a fire
going in the almost burned-out stove, brewed up
some bear huntin' coffee, and sat dunking
cookies, impatiently waiting for first light.
The cabin only had one small window and I
would douse the candle every so often and peer
out the opening, looking in vain for the first
hints of dawn.

When I could finally see a little glow to the
east, I grabbed my rifle, daypack, flashlight,
and out the door I went. The first part of the
trail went past a bear mark tree with wear holes
in the ground. This mark tree and twist holes
had been established by grizzlies as a response
to the cabin being built beside the main bear
trail. The wear holes were spaced in such a way
that it was awkward to walk in them; they
weren't designed for a man's stride. I hiked
down below the Gyllenspetz confluence (it
came in on the other side of the river) to a

shallow ripple where I could cross.

I sat down at the bottom of a bank, well below the trail, in a spot I felt was safe from a bear walking up behind me. I had a few small bushes in front of me for camouflage when daylight arrived. I planned to wait for good light as I would have to take off my pants and boots and use a stabilizer stick to cross the river in order to hunt the Gyllenspetz slough. I had done this before, but when you are by yourself in the bush, you have to do river crossings very carefully.

After about a half-hour it was getting light enough to make out shapes of flood debris on the opposing river bar. I thought I had heard noises on the other side, but I wasn't sure because of the continuous gurgling river noise. Then I heard the clear guttural bawl of a cub. I squinted and thought I could see a small dark shape scurrying about. Five minutes later I could make out the shape of a sow and two small cubs near the river's edge, upstream from me about 40 metres. I had tested the wind several times, and there was a steady, cold, down-river breeze.

In another 20 minutes it was almost bright daylight; I was enjoying watching this bear family interact and going about the business of survival. The sow had caught three separate Coho salmon in a small upstream side slough, and each time she had brought the fish back downstream into the open gravel bar. She kept looking up the Gyllenspetz Creek and every few minutes would stand up on her hind legs to sniff the air.

I was starting to think that somehow she was sensing me, but I couldn't see how that was possible because I was down-wind and out of sight. The cubs were oblivious to their mother's concern and kept trying to pull the latest fish out from under her paws. She would gently cuff them when they became too annoying. Every so often a cub would grab a chunk of fish skin in its mouth and take off running with its sibling in hot pursuit. These chases would end in a wrestling match, and as soon as one of the cubs let out a bawl, the sow was there in an instant to make sure everything was okay.

After one of these chase, wrestling, bawl, and instant-check episodes, the three bears were walking back to the remains of the last fish. The cubs were ahead of the sow and almost to the fish when the sow stood up on her hind legs and looked at the brush line to her right. I saw a flash of black come out of the brush and head directly for the cubs. The sow was about ten metres from the cubs; she let out a horrific growl and started an angling run trying to head off the large boar.

She made contact with the male about two metres from the cubs and tried to bite him in the flank. He ignored her, and as he passed by her I could see that he was a good foot taller than she was. The cubs didn't even know what was going on when the male grabbed one by the middle of the back and slammed it against the ground. The sow had been knocked flat by her impact with the male but recovered instantly and was just about to jump on his back when he spun around and hit her on top of her head with his right front paw. She had seen the blow coming and tried to dodge sideways. The glancing blow drove her face into the gravel and the momentum of her run caused her whole body to upend over her head, like a cartwheel. I figured that her neck must have been broken.

The other cub had run down the river bar about 50 metres and stood there bawling. The male put his left front paw on the wounded cub that

was lying by the river's edge bawling and trying to move. The boar used his canine teeth to
open up the cub's stomach area and grabbed a
mouthful of intestines, then reared back, pulling out about a metre of rupturing guts. The cub
was squirming and making gurgling sounds.

I was somewhat in a state of shock and
couldn't fathom what I was watching. I had
already put a shell in the chamber, but I just sat
there, dumbfounded, and didn't move.

I could see that the sow had serious damage to
her head. I could also see her rib cage going up
and down in irregular movements. Her head,
neck, and chest were covered with blood.

The large boar fed on the cub for about two
minutes. The surviving cub went silent and
started walking in a wide semicircle towards
its mother. The male had his back to the sow
and the other cub that had slowly walked to
within about ten metres of its mother. The cub
put its head down and whimpered. The boar
spun around and was on top of the cub in about
four bounds. The cub tried a desperate run
towards the creek but stumbled over a small
log.

The boar came to a sudden stop when he seized
the cub's head with his mouth. He put both front
feet on the cub's chest and pulled up, severing
the neck spinal column. The head was just
hanging by stretched skin.

The sow sat up on her haunches with her front
legs dangling in front of her, and tried to look
around. Her right eye seemed intact, and she
finally seemed to focus on the boar, but she
didn't move or make any sound. She sat like
that for a minute, then slowly leaned forward
and stood up on all fours. Her head was low,
with her bloody nose almost touching the
ground. I could now see that the boar's claws

had made a ragged scalping of the whole back left side of her head, and a flap of skin, including the ear, was hanging down covering her left eye. All of a sudden she took off for the brush where the boar had come out. The big black male casually turned and watched her go, then returned to feeding on the cub.

I'll never forget what happened next. I can close my eyes and picture the scene as if it were yesterday. The boar turned away from the cub and started walking towards the carcass of the other cub. He went into a heads-high posture and walked with a swagger while twisting his front feet inward with each step. He was doing some kind of strut, and it seemed to be some important behaviour in relation to what he had just accomplished. As he strutted up to the other cub, I could barely see what looked like urine being intermittently shot from his penis at about every other step.

The boar was starting to feed again on the first cub when my bullet pierced his hide just above the point of the shoulder. It went through the shoulder blade on a long angle and slammed into the backbone right at the hump. His back-end collapsed straight down, then his front end fell over sideways away from me. He lifted his head slightly and was trying to get up when the second bullet tore through his left lung and lodged under the skin by the spine. The third bullet passed through his heart and right lung, exiting out through his back.

When I left the Talchako two days later I was still uncomfortable with what I had witnessed. Not because of the death and destruction; I had already seen plenty of death at that point in my life. I was left with a slightly hollow feeling in my chest because at that time in my life I was a natural regimist. This event was a capper on a series of experiences I had had in nature that were contrary to my belief system. I had given up on mankind many years before and wanted a nature that was much better than man.

I now know that mankind, even at its ugliest, reflects nature. The territorial warfare of Jane Goodall's chimpanzees, the endless past extinctions, the brute competition at every level, the cannibalism, rape, and murder, it's all there in nature if you dare to look. But amidst all the horror is beauty, serenity, care, and love. That sow grizzly that tried valiantly to save her children will always have a special place in my heart, and I no longer hold a grudge towards those male grizzlies that are acting out an age-old, genetically programmed behavioural requirement.

1 0

Polar Bears

When I started this book, I did not intend to include
a section on polar bears. About half-way through the
first draft, I received a telephone call from Tom
Juhasz, who is the Seagoing Support Supervisor for
the Ocean Physics Section of the Institute of Ocean
Sciences, Department of Fisheries and Oceans
(D.F.O.), at Sidney, B.C.

He had heard about the bear defense training I had
done for the D.F.O. Biological Research Station at
Nanaimo, B.C. and wanted to know about the possibility of a training course for his group. We talked
about the training and possible dates. He then asked
me if I had a polar bear segment in my training as
some of his staff would be working in the Arctic in
the near future. I told him that I did not feel qualified
to speak on polar bears as I had never encountered
one. He felt it was important that I provide him and
his colleagues with polar bear information as well as
information about grizzlies and black bears, so I told
him that I would do research on polar bears for his
group, and we decided to do the training the following year.

In January of 1993, I gave a talk about bear hazard
safety to a group of people at the annual safety semi-
nar of the B.C./Yukon Chamber of Mines in Vancouver, B.C. After my talk, a woman by the name of
Helen Thayer gave a presentation about her solo trek

to the magnetic North Pole. She was the first woman to accomplish this task, and at the age of 50.

Helen started life in New Zealand and was fortunate enough to be born to parents who were active outdoors people. At a very young age she became involved in winter sports and mountain climbing. Her hero was Sir Edmund Hillary, a fellow New Zealander, and she wanted to accomplish some noteworthy things in her own life.

Helen competed in international sports but eventually returned to her first love, mountain climbing. She climbed some of the highest peaks in South America, Russia, and China, and often dreamed about a trek to the magnetic pole; not just a trek, but a solo trek on skis with all her supplies trailing behind her in a sled.

Eventually ending up in the United States, Helen met and married her husband, Bill. In time, Bill shared her enthusiasm about the adventure she longed for, and he helped her plan her Arctic trip. Finally, in March of 1988, the time had come, and Helen flew from Vancouver, B.C. to Resolute Bay in the Northwest Territories (N.W.T.).

The Inuit people at Resolute Bay could not believe what Helen intended to do; they warned her that she would not survive the polar bears. She spent two weeks with the Inuit, learning the ways of the ice. Eventually, Tony, an Inuit polar bear hunter, convinced Helen to take a dog with her which he would gladly supply. As it turned out, it's lucky that she accepted Tony's offer and took 'Charlie' with her.

The following excerpt from Helen's book, *Polar Dream* (1993), Simon & Schuster, demonstrates the difficulty in dealing with polar bears who are in the "hunting mode":

. . .

   Last to be packed was the tent.   I was

completely engrossed in finding a way to twist
the tent ice screws out of the ice so that my
hands wouldn't scream in protest when suddenly I heard a deep, long growl coming from
the depths of Charlie's throat. In a flash I
looked at him and then in the direction in
which he was staring. I knew what I would see
even before I looked. A polar bear!

It was a female followed by two cubs coming
from Bathurst Island, slowly, purposefully,
plodding through the rough shore ice toward
me. They were two hundred yards away. With
a pounding heart I grabbed my loaded rifle and
flare gun and carefully walked sideways a few
steps to Charlie, who was snarling with a sav-
agery that caught my breath. Without taking
my eyes off the bear, I unclipped Charlie from
his ice anchor and, again walking sideways, I
led him to the sled where I clipped his chain to a
tie-down rope. The bear, now only 150 yards
away, wasn't stopping. Her cubs had dropped
back but she came on with a steady measured
stride while I frantically tried to remember all
the Inuit had told me. Keep eye contact, move
sideways or slightly forward, never backward,
stay calm, don't show fear, stand beside a tent,
sled, or other large object to make my five feet
three inches appear as large as possible. Don't
shoot unless forced to. Don't wound a bear,
you'll make it even more dangerous, and
never run. Repeating to myself, "Stay calm,
stay calm," I fired a warning shot to the bear's
left. The loud explosion of the .338 had no
effect. On she came. I fired a flare, landing it
a little to her right. Her head moved slightly in
its direction but she didn't stop. I fired another
flare, this time dropping it right in front of her.
She stopped, looked at the flare burning a bright
red on the white ice, then looked at me. She was

only one hundred feet away now.

By this time my nerves were as tight as violin strings and my heart could have been heard at base camp. The bear began to step around the flare, and I dropped another flare two feet in front of her. Again she stopped, looked at the flare and at me. Then she fixed her tiny black eyes on Charlie, who was snarling trying to reach her. She looked back at her cubs. I could sense her concern about Charlie's snarling, rabid act and her cubs. She waited for her cubs to catch up, then moved to my left in a half circle. In spite of my sore fingers I fired two more flares in quick succession, trying to draw a line between her and me. She stopped, then moved back toward my right. I fired two more flares and again she stopped. She seemed to want to cross the line of flares but was unsure of the result and of Charlie, so she elected to stay back. She kept moving right in a half circle, still one hundred feet away. Finally, with a last long look she plodded north with her two new cubs trotting behind her, their snow-white coats contrasting with their mother's creamy, pale yellow color.

The whole episode lasted fifteen minutes but seemed years long. I was a nervous wreck. My hands were shaking as I stood still holding my rifle and flare gun, watching the trio slowly move north. But in spite of the mind-numbing fear that still gripped me, I could feel deep down inside a real satisfaction. I now knew that I could stand up to a bear in the wild, stay calm enough to function and still remember the words of wisdom from the Inuit. With Charlie's help I had passed my first test. The bear had been completely silent as it had approached and moved around me on paws thickly padded with fur on the undersides. I was thankful for Charlie's warning. Now he had stopped growling and snarling but still stood rigid, watching the bears as they zigzagged in and out of the rough ice hunting for the seals that lived in the cold waters beneath the ice. He seemed to hardly notice the giant hug I gave him. He was still on guard.

The bears were only about four hundred yards away but I decided to continue packing my tent and move around to stay warm, still keeping a wary eye on the bears. I was getting cold. My fear and flowing adrenaline had kept me warm but I was beginning to shiver now. I finished packing and stood around until ten o'clock, keeping warm, until I was sure the bears had disappeared and weren't circling back to me. If I stayed out from the coast, keeping away from the rough ice, I hoped to make up the time I had lost. But as I started out I still thought about the bears. Even as frightened as I had been, it was a thrill to see a bear and her cubs in their natural environment. She was unafraid of me, powerful and dangerous, yet graceful. And she was a tender, attentive mother caring for her cubs.

All went well for the next hour. As usual I tried to look for bears in all directions at once. Being alone, I had to keep a 360-degree watch. The sky was still clear with just a light wind coming from the north. It was bitterly cold and my blue neoprene mask was developing a thick layer of ice where my breath froze. I could see Kalivik Island two miles northeast. I should be well past the island by nightfall.

Suddenly I noticed movement about four hundred yards away to the southeast. Surely not another bear. My nerves weren't yet ready for a second encounter. But a moment later there was no doubt. It was a bear. It was downwind from us, and Charlie hadn't picked up its scent. As fast as I could, I released my skis, again grabbed my rifle and flare gun, and attached Charlie to the sled rope. I stood waiting with Charlie at my side. He was watching, his body rigid and his back hair standing on end, eyes fixed on the approaching bear, but he was silent. In a voice that was anything but calm, I said, "Why don't you growl? Do something, Charlie." But then I sensed that his silence was a signal to me. He knew something that I didn't know. So I too, stood silent, watching, not moving, with only the sound of my pounding heart in my ears.

This bear was a very large, powerful male, the same creamy white as the first bear, and he was moving toward us at a faster pace. His head was held low and he walked with a typical polar bear pigeon-toed gait. He stopped to raise his black nose, his head moving slowly back and forth as he caught our scent, then he lowered his head and walked on again. Charlie was at the end of his chain, still silent, except for an occasional, short, low growl. Then as the bear came to within 250 feet, Charlie fell completely silent again. There was something different about this bear and he knew it.

The Inuit had warned me not to show fear. But I couldn't just stand there and tell myself I wasn't afraid. I was terrified. So I tried replacing my fear with aggressive thoughts. "I have as much right to be here as this bear," I said to myself. "He has no right to invade my space." It sounded ridiculous but it worked. Instead of shrinking to a defensive position, I began to feel that I had at least some control over the situation.

Now the bear was only 150 feet way. I fired one warning shot to the left, then two flares in quick succession. He kept coming toward me, very deliberate and more aggressive in his movements than the first bear. I quickly fired three more flares, each one landing in front of him. It was time for Charlie to use his bear-chasing skills.

My thumb was on the collar clip when Charlie suddenly leaped three feet in the air at the end of his chain with a loud snarling growl that set my right eardrum ringing. The bear stopped in his tracks, took one long look and, as I fired more flares, slowly retreated to our left. Charlie was once again silent. So I took the cue and stood silently at his side. I watched as the bear moved away in a wide sweeping arc, looking back over his shoulder now and then. He had been impressed by Charlie's leaping attack and was leaving reluctantly. My worry now was whether he would return.

Sure enough, at about three hundred yards he stopped and turned to face us. He paused for a few moments as if contemplating the situation, then started back with the same quick, determined pigeon-toed walk as before. This was too much. The pit of my stomach was an ice cube, even my knees were shaking. We had to get rid of this bear somehow, but I was undecided about whether to let Charlie go so he could deal with the bear or to try to shoot to kill.

The bear was still two hundred yards away, so I decided to fire a last warning shot and flares before taking more drastic action. I fired the .338 but I could tell by now that these bears were not very impressed by the loud cannonlike explosion, so I began laying out flares as fast as I could, thankful that I had bought a supply large enough to do an army proud. All at once the bear bent down and touched a hot, burning flare with his nose. He threw his head in the air, rolled on the ice, got up as quickly as a cat, then moved out as fast as he had arrived. It was with heartfelt relief that I stood watching him disappear. He didn't even bother to look over his shoulder this time.

After two encounters with bears in one day, I needed to stop to regroup and have something to eat and drink. I had a severe case of the shakes and I was beginning to wonder if my nerves could stand much more of this abuse.

I hugged Charlie long and hard. He had helped me twice in one day. "Thank you, Charlie," I said. I fed him some crackers, and as I ate my share I wondered again at the different moods Charlie had shown when facing these two bears. There was much for me to learn out here. Tony had been right when he told me to keep Charlie tethered until I needed him to chase a bear. That way I had control over him and he would be there at the precise moment I needed him. Charlie was leaning on my leg begging for more crackers. I didn't have much appetite. I felt as if I had just survived a head-on collision with a freight train. I gave Charlie my crackers. He had no problem with his appetite. This polar bear business was fun to him.

* * *

I introduced you to Peter Clarkson in Note #2 at the end of the *Bear Aggressive Behaviour* chapter. Peter is the Wolf/Grizzly Biologist for the Dept. of Renewable Resources in the N.W.T. He has been with the N.W.T. Government for nine years and originally came from Alberta.

Peter has done considerable work with grizzly bears and has a very balanced perspective about trying to come up with good strategies for protecting both people and bears. Some of the most interesting work he has done is the study of deterrence techniques against polar bears. This work was done at Churchill, Manitoba.

Peter teaches bear safety courses and is responsible for putting together some of the best "Safety in Bear Country" material that I have seen.

Ian Sterling is known as "Mr. Polar Bear". He works for the Canadian Wildlife Service in Edmonton, Alberta. This gentleman has studied polar bears in about every way you can imagine and has been at it for a long time. He has made a significant contribution to the understanding of polar bear biology and how best to protect this species.

Peter and Ian have recently put together an up-dated version of material for polar bear damage prevention and control methods. This is an excellent piece of information that brings together biological and practical strategies for reducing human/polar bear conflict. This material will be published in the near future in the United States Department of Agriculture (U.S.D.A.) *Prevention and Control of Wildlife Damage* manual.

I am not a polar bear expert, but if you are going to work or travel in polar bear country, I would suggest that you obtain the following three publications and read them in the numbered order:

1. *SAFETY IN BEAR COUNTRY*, A Reference Manual, by the Dept. of Renewable Resources, N.W.T. Government. This manual gives excellent information about all three species of North American bears and bear country safety techniques.

2. *POLAR DREAM*, by Helen Thayer. This book has repeated accounts of polar bear encoun-

ters and it demonstrates how difficult it can be to see a stalking polar bear under some circumstances. It also shows how difficult it can be to determine whether a polar bear is just curious or wanting you for a meal, and the importance of a good polar bear dog. Helen's main system of deterrence was the use of a flare pistol.

3. *U.S.D.A., PREVENTION AND CONTROL OF WILDLIFE DAMAGE* manual. This manual has good technical detail in all aspects of dealing with polar bears.

Polar bears are closely related to and recently speciated from, grizzly bears. They are not as defensive-aggressive as grizzly bears and can be quite tolerant of each other. Their predatory behaviour, however, is far more direct and defined than that of the black bear. Polar bears have evolved back to a truly predatory bear, and must be dealt with as such.

Helen Thayer's book indicates a higher level of predatory aggression in polar bears than the work done by Peter and Ian. I asked Helen about this discrepancy. She stated that when you encounter polar bears on land, or if you are on a snowmobile, or with a dog team or other people, these bears respond differently. She explained that her polar bear experiences were one-on-one encounters on sea ice.

Helen Thayer's book shows the worst case potential of polar bear predatory behaviour. If you go to the Arctic, you will most likely be there under circumstances that would relate to the more average aspect of polar bear predatory behaviour as indicated in the scientific work. But the policy I always follow with bears, and I'm sure Peter and Ian would agree, is this: Plan for the worst-case scenario.

I am going to outline the basic encounter strategies of Helen Thayer's book, which come from Inuit defense strategies and her own experience with polar bears. I will then outline the strategies from Peter and Ian's work.

From *Polar Dream* by Helen Thayer:

1. Expect every polar bear you encounter to be capable of hunting and killing you.
2. Stay facing an approaching or circling bear and maintain eye contact.
3. Stay standing in an encounter - polar bears are attracted to anything looking like a seal (i.e. a supine human!).
4. If you're by yourself, use a flare gun to deter a bear, and keep the defense firearm ready.
5. After you have deterred a bear, expect it to circle, follow, and try you again. (Carefully watch behind you for several hours after an encounter.)
6. If more than one person is in a party, stand about 20 feet apart in an encounter. If the bear starts zeroing in on and approaching one person, you are too far apart.
7. Polar bears will sometimes ambush you from behind ice mounds or other types of concealment.
8. A thin-looking bear that plods directly towards you with its head down is very dangerous and hard to deter.
9. Young sub-adult bears act nervous and are unsure of themselves.
10. Flares should arc through the air and land in front of the bear. Considerable practice is required to achieve this ability.
11. A bear will stop and turn sideways when reassessing a predatory approach.
12. The best way to save both people and bear lives is with the use of a good polar bear dog on a leash.

The two manuals that I have listed above (that contain Peter's, Ian's, and other biologists' work) have considerable information about camp set-up, detection systems, and capture and transport information. I am going to outline just their material on polar bear avoidance, deterrence, and defense strategies:

1. Use bear monitors (armed look-out guards) to detect and deter bears around camps and work areas.

2. Use chained or leashed dogs for detecting and deterring bears. (Must be a properly trained, alert dog.)

3. Reduce or eliminate (if possible) food or garbage smells as they can draw polar bears from long distances.

4. Keep snow removed from around buildings and tents, and have area well lit.

5. Never stick your head out of a tent, or walk out of a building, if there is a possibility that a polar bear may be standing right there. (Polar bears specialize in attacking emerging seals.)

6. Watch for and be aware of bear sign.

7. When travelling, carefully examine the route ahead with binoculars - remember that polar bears can be difficult to see in blowing snow and in other reduced visual conditions.

8. Travel in daylight and avoid traveling in twilight or dark.

9. Use warning shots, cracker shells, thunder flashes, flares, birdscare cartridges, and air horns for deterrence. Also use snowmobiles and other motorized equipment for bear deterrence around camps.

10. Pepper spray may not work in some Arctic conditions, and no testing of its effectiveness with polar bears has been done.

11. Use "the three slug system" for polar bears:

First round - cracker shell, second round - plastic slug, third round - lead slug. Only use this system when there is a second firearm for back-up with all lead rounds.
12. If it's unavoidable, kill the bear with lead rounds to chest from 12-gauge pump shotgun or high-powered rifle (30-06 and up).

It is extremely important that you read the original sources for the above outlines as I have condensed the material significantly:

SAFETY IN BEAR COUNTRY (1992) A Reference Manual. Dept. of Renewable Resources, Government of the N. W. T., Inuvik, North West Territories, Canada X0E 0T0

POLAR DREAM (1993) by Helen Thayer, Simon & Schuster, obtain from Village Books, 1210 11th St. Bellingham, Wash. U.S.A. 98225

PREVENTION AND CONTROL OF WILD-LIFE DAMAGE manual, U.S.D.A. Wildlife Damage Handbook, 202 Natural Resources Hall, University of Nebraska, Lincoln NE 68583-0819.

The flare pistol that Helen Thayer used for deterring polar bears was a 12-gauge signal pistol, brand OLIN. The flares were 12-gauge red meteor flares obtained from marine supply stores.

For additional reading I would strongly recommend:

POLAR BEARS (1988) by Ian Stirling, University of Michigan Press, Ann Arbor, Michigan, U.S.A.

Black bear looking at mark tree near Atnarko River, Bella Coola Valley. *Courtesy Stefan Himmer*

Sub-adult grizzly bear walking on bear trail in upper Bella Coola Valley. *Courtesy Stefan Himmer*

Spraying bear at three metres from behind tree.

Gary Shelton

Spray drifts sideways at about two and a half metres with an
eight kilometre per hour cross-wind. *Gary Shelton*

In a predatory encounter, ready spray, then threaten bear with limb, or whatever is available. In a defensive-aggressive encounter, ready spray and back up slowly if possible.

Gary Shelton

If defensive system fails, in a defensive-aggressive attack, roll up in a tight ball and protect face and back of neck. Always fight back if attack seems to be predatory.

Gary Shelton

Sow grizzly with second-year cub on bear trail by Atnarko
River, Bella Coola Valley.   *Courtesy Stefan Himmer*

Look closely at this picture and determine whether it is a
grizzly or black bear.   *Courtesy Stefan Himmer*

Discussing shotgun jamming problems during firearms training. *Gary Shelton*

Stress testing firearms trainee with moving target.
Bear on preceeding page is a grizzly. *Gary Shelton*

Beautiful Bella Coola Valley, paradise for both man and bear.
Gary Shelton

Bud Lorenzen on bear migration trail in Talchako River Valley. *Gary Shelton*

Author standing by black bear den in hollow of large cedar tree, found by Randy Svisdahl.　　　*Courtesy Ian Douglas*

- PART II -

11

Bear Management

The previous chapters have provided practical information on how to reduce danger in a bear encounter. The remainder of this book will show how to reduce the number of dangerous bear encounters by using proper bear management.

Reducing human/bear conflict is a double-edged sword; we must teach people how to try to avoid bear encounters and how to reduce their impact on bears, but we must also manage bear populations and individual bears in a manner that will reduce the danger and impact on people.

I must now add support to the first part of this book.

During the last five years I have seen considerable misinformation about bears spread out on the table of public debate, most of it orchestrated by people with a burning cause and an agenda to ram forward. The most damaging types of misinformation I have seen are the beautifully presented T.V. documentaries about bears being endangered. The researchers for these projects have followed a prescribed and biased story line by picking and choosing those bear studies or biologists who will project the agenda. People who are unfamiliar with all bear studies, and who do not know that scientific enquiry is an oscillating process of challenge and debate, can easily be misled.

I am going to carefully limit myself here to topics that will directly or indirectly affect human/bear conflict or bear conservation. I must deal with these remaining issues to insure that you have a complete knowledge of all factors that relate to the subject of this book. The way in which we manage bears will definitely influence how many people are killed and injured by bears in B.C. over the next 20 years. The following information and views pertain to B.C. only and may or may not apply to other areas of North America.

LOGGING

Some of our TV pseudo-scientists are claiming that logging is destroying bears. This is only slightly true. Logging access can destroy bears if hunting regulations are not temporarily changed to reduce the impact, and massive clearcuts can have an impact on bears. The truth is, in many of our mature timber stands, logging creates excellent bear forage, and logging is presently contributing to increased sub-adult survival rates in many areas of the province, particularly in the northern interior.

Most people have heard about the Bowron clearcut. It is so huge that it can be seen by orbiting astronauts in outer space. It is an ugly scar that is slowly regenerating. What a lot of people don't know is that this large slash has caused a significant increase in wildlife populations in the area, especially black bears.

In timbered areas, bears obtain most of their food from regenerating sites (burns, slides, logging slash, etc.) and from old-growth where the canopy has opened up. Second-growth and mature stands have very little bear food in them. People in many areas of the province who take my bear safety courses tell me that the bear population is increasing, and that many of their bear sightings are in slow

Coastal old-growth forest system with semi-open canopy.
There is considerable bear food here.   *Gary Shelton*

regenerating logging slashes.

The level of timber harvest in B.C. prior to 1980 created a mosaic of regeneration and old-growth that

Coastal mature forest (middle-aged). No bear food here at all.   *Gary Shelton*

was beneficial to bears, and logging, in many ways, replaced fire as the rejuvenator of the forest. The higher level of harvest during the 1980s, however,

Five-year-old coastal logging slash. This slash will provide
excellent bear food for 15 years or more.   *Gary Shelton*

will have a long-term detrimental effect on bears for
two reasons: First, there will eventually be too much
second-growth plantation timber that will be

harvested before it becomes old-growth. Second,
present restocking techniques shorten the herbaceous
regeneration cycle.

The present reductions in timber harvesting being
initiated around the province and the setting aside of
wilderness areas will help bears in some areas, but
we are now going too far with this concept. For 29
years I have observed the way in which bears utilize
logged areas: as long as the timber harvest levels
are not too high, the critical habitat is protected, and
the road access restricted if necessary, bears do fine
with logging.

BEAR VIEWING

Four years ago, when the National Geographic Soci-
ety released its excellent grizzly bear film showing
people photographing brown bears at McNeil River
Falls, Alaska, I knew I was going to have problems.
At that time I was Chairman of the Central Coast
Grizzly Management Committee, which had members from all government ministries and organizations that were interested in grizzly management.

The provincial government was trying to identify
potential bear viewing areas in B.C. for major tourist attraction sites. Several years earlier the federal
government had built a salmon spawning channel
on the lower Atnarko River in South Tweedsmuir
Park. The spawning channel was starting to attract
grizzlies and some parks personnel were suggesting
that this area had potential as a bear viewing site.

Later that year, when I was travelling through Williams Lake, B.C., I stopped and talked to management personnel in the regional office of B.C. Parks.
I asked them if they were considering the Atnarko
spawning channel as a possible bear viewing spot;
they said yes, they were. I presented the following
argument as to why this plan would not work.

The McNeil River bears are habituated to human

presence in a very controlled and special way. This special type of habituation would not be possible with the existing road access on the Atnarko.

The McNeil River bears do not interact with a local human settlement. The Atnarko bears do, and they also encounter people on park trails.

The McNeil River bears have a learned behaviour of tolerance towards other bears (and probably people) because of the open-habitat conditions and abundance of fish. The Atnarko River bears of South Tweedsmuir Park are coastal jungle bears that are much more reactive in their defensive-aggressive behaviour.

A bear viewing station on the Atnarko would habituate bears to human presence and significantly increase the human/bear conflict in a community where too many bears are already killed each year in order to maintain public safety.

The parks managers in Williams Lake accepted my argument and that was the end of bear viewing on the Atnarko.

I'm sure there are a few places in the province where bear viewing may be possible. However, it will have to be done very carefully in order to protect the safety of both people and bears in the area.

BEAR PARTS TRADE

There has been so much misinformation presented on bear parts trade in B.C. that this subject deserves a lengthy exploration.

I recently read a book sponsored by a prestigious world preservationist organization (that I used to support). In the section on bears, the author described the trade in bear parts taking place in various parts of the world, and then used every rumor and innuendo possible to indicate that hunters and poachers were decimating bear populations in B.C. for parts.

I was somewhat surprised to what level this person

and organization would stoop to push their cause. The author tried to explain bear aggressive behaviour by dismissing it as a usual response to people making mistakes with bears. That was irritating enough, but he then went on to do something very irresponsible. He felt obliged to mention black bear predatory behaviour, but stated that such behaviour was extremely "rare" and that Herrero had devised a defense strategy for this behaviour that resolved the problem. It is amazing what some people will say and do in order to protect bears, especially when they themselves are not at risk.

There has been a lot of frantic material presented to the B.C. public about bears being slaughtered at a horrific rate for bear parts in order to supply the Asian black market. This is an exaggeration of what is actually going on. There are bears being killed for parts, all right, but the past and present levels are not high enough to even come close to threatening bear populations.

There are other places in the world (mainly China and India) where bear parts trade is seriously endangering bear species. In countries where many people barely make a living, the value of selling black market contraband usually outweighs the penalty of being caught. Bear parts in B.C., however, would have to become much more valuable than even the exaggerated claims of some groups before we would have a serious problem.

It has been legal to sell bear parts in B.C. for a long time. This trade has slowly grown over the years, but in the last six years it grew significantly. Because of B.C.'s location and its export activity, and the growing demand for bear gall bladders, wildlife managers became concerned about this trade during the 1980s. In 1990 a law was passed that required all buyers of bear gall bladders to have a fur trader's licence, and to make monthly reports of their purchase and sell volumes using the existing

fur-trader returns. For the first time this gave the
Ministry of Environment the ability to monitor gall
bladder trade.

After a few years of monitoring, some Conservation
Officers (C.O.s) became convinced that an unscru-
pulous buyer could easily buy and sell many bladders - both legal and illegal - and only show a part of
the actual volume in fur-trader returns. Sting operations were set up and some arrests were made. In
one highly publicized arrest two years ago, the buyer
had about 200 galls, the majority of which were taken
from *legally* killed bears, but the buyer did have
some illegal galls, including the one he bought from
the undercover C.O. But this buyer did not have his
fur-trader reports in order, so most of these galls
were illegal, from a paper work point of view.

On February 1st, 1993 the B.C. Government's new
ban on bear parts came into effect. This law forbids
the possession, trafficking, import, and export of
bear galls, paws, and genitalia. Since the ban has
been in place, more arrests have been made, and one
case involved 100 illegal galls. It would be almost
impossible to determine what portion of those 100
galls came from legal hunter-kill bears, or resident
control-kill bears, versus bears that were killed
solely for parts. It is possible that most of the galls
were from parts-killed bears, but unlikely.

While researching this subject, I talked to three
C.O.s who have spent considerable time working on
this problem. I also talked to many people in the
operations aspect of the Ministry of Environment,
taxidermists, guides, hunters, and many others.

The only bear part for which there is significant
demand is gall bladders. Contrary to existing misinformation, our C.O. Service has found almost no
black market in B.C. for bear paws, and only a
small market for black bear claws. One taxidermist
told me that during the six years he legally sold bear
gall bladders (from hunter kills), he repeatedly tried

to sell bear paws to Korean buyers. He sold a few, for $5 a pair, and as far as he could tell they were either consumed by the buyer himself or given away as gifts. Black bear claws bring about $10 each.

Bear galls sell for a pretty good price, but nothing like the amounts you will find in some supposedly prestigious publications that twist weights and prices in a way that is ridiculous. The average gall bladder weighs about 45-50 grams. During the late 1980s, the first seller would get between $80-$150 per gall. The buyer would then sell to an exporter for $200-$500 per gall. After that the value was based on what country the gall ended up in. In some Asian countries the price doubled; in others, where there are severe penalties for bear parts trade, the price skyrocketed. People distort bear parts information by quoting the price of gall bladders in certain countries, then implying that that price is paid to poachers in B.C.

In the past, there were many black bears killed through resident control action, and after the kill someone removed the gall bladder. Anyone who finds such a carcass assumes that the bear was originally killed for parts only.

There is sufficient evidence to state that prior to the ban, there were 200-300 black bears killed for parts in B.C. per year. There is even some evidence that as many as 500-800 black bears were killed per year for parts. Some Conservation Officers believe that the number was as high as 1,500. I do not personally believe that the actual kill of black bears, solely for parts, has ever exceeded about 500 bears per year. There are very few grizzly bears being killed for parts - probably less than 20 per year.

Most C.O.s feel that the bear parts trade is not threatening bears, but that a constant effort must be made to keep it under control. The bear parts ban has given them a significant, much-needed tool for dealing with this problem.

I have not always felt that a bear parts ban was needed in B.C., but there is another important reason for the ban: On a world-wide scale, the B.C. ban will significantly help law enforcement agencies in other countries who intercept bear parts from countries where the parts trade is endangering bears. Smugglers will no longer be able to claim that their contraband is legal B.C. parts. You can imagine how many phony B.C. export permits have been used to move illegal parts around the world.

We do not yet know for sure how successful the bear parts ban will be. There is some evidence that the black market price for galls in B.C. has jumped. But I believe the ban will reduce the total annual kill for parts well below 300. Even though our Conservation Officer Service has always been understaffed and under-funded, I am confident that the regular C.O.s and the new undercover unit will be able to keep a handle on this problem. There is one thing that could really help them in their efforts: All British Columbians should keep their eyes and ears open for bear parts trade activity. If you see or hear anything suspicious, call your local C.O. Service and let them know about it.

Most hunters I know are happy about the bear parts ban because they have been targeted and blamed for some of the trade by radical preservationists. The truth is that hunters and taxidermists are the two groups of people that bear parts buyers must approach if they are going to obtain large volumes of parts, and contrary to what some people claim, these two groups will not tolerate bears being killed for that reason.

There will always be some bears killed in B.C. for parts by poachers. But the number of bears killed for parts will average far less from now on than the number of bears killed through control actions (both C.O. and resident) for protection of human property and life.

CONTROL KILLS

In recent years B.C. has experienced a significant increase in human population growth. Much of this growth has been in suburban and rural areas. This human population increase, coupled with more bears - because we now protect them better - means more human/bear conflict in many areas of the province.

In 1992, Conservation Officers in B.C. responded to 1,479 black bear complaints and 80 grizzly bear complaints. There were 248 black bears re-located, and 579 were killed. In addition, 13 grizzly bears were re located, and 28 were killed. This does not include park data. That was a bad year and the average control kill would usually be more like 400 black bears and 20 grizzlies.

In my opinion, the number of Conservation Officer (C.O.) control kills per year is equal to the approximate number of bears killed by B.C. residents in defense of property or life - for a total average of about 800 black bears and 40 grizzlies. Twenty years ago residents would have killed two or three times more bears through control actions than C.O.s.

The majority of these resident control kills go unreported as most British Columbians are afraid they will be charged, even for a legitimate kill. The majority of resident control kills are legitimate, but there are of course some people who kill bears for little or no provocation. But they are the minority.

Typically, bear kill numbers move up and down in a wave fashion where there is considerable conflict going on. The bear population builds up, human tolerance goes down, and ·a two-or three-year kill-off takes place, then there's a six-to seven-year calm before the next build-up. Quite often during the calm periods, people make the mistake of thinking that the problems have been solved.

British Columbians have made significant headway in the last ten years in reducing food and garbage availability for bears, both in small communities and in parks. But there is a limit as to how much headway can be made in that type of conflict. If the bear population is high, and at some point in the year the available food is low, there will be major conflict no matter what people do. But it is everyone's responsibility to eliminate compost, garbage, and food availability for bears wherever possible.

If the present pressure to protect bears more and more continues, our Conservation Officer Service will become nothing more than a bear killing machine with little time to devote towards other problems. Anyone who believes that B.C. rural residents can live safely and economically with bear populations at maximum levels, simply does not have a clue what human/bear conflict really involves.

BEAR POPULATIONS

About two years ago, a researcher for one of the biggest environmental groups in Western Canada called me and wanted to know what I knew about the grizzly population on the Atnarko River. He had received a report that fisheries personnel had only seen one grizzly on the river that year, and he assumed that there was only one left. I told him that there were about 60 to 70 bears in that area, that the population was rising, and that the Central Coast grizzlies were doing fine.

A month later this organization released a public statement saying they had obtained a Ministry of Environment inter-ministry memo showing that the Wildlife Branch had increased the estimate of grizzly bears in the Province from 6,600 to 11,500. They claimed that this increase in the population estimate was due to pressure from hunters and guides who wanted to justify the existing grizzly kill. They went on to state that this meant that grizzlies were being harvested at an annual rate of 20% in B.C.

It's too bad this organization didn't relate their statement to the previous 15 years' hunter kill numbers and to grizzly reproductive rates. They would have discovered that according to their claim, grizzlies in B.C. should have been extinct four years before they uncovered this terrible conspiracy.

Unfortunately this incident hurt the very people who have done the most to protect bears. The reason that the Wildlife Branch increased the estimate for the grizzly population was due to overwhelming evidence coming in from all quarters that their estimate at that time was extremely low. The Ministry of Environment presently estimates the grizzly population at between 10,000 and 13,000, and black bears at about 140,000. I believe that both of these estimates are still quite conservative.

The average hunter kill for black bears (both resident and guided hunters) in B.C. is 4,200. The black bear control kill averages 800 (C.O. and resident), and bear parts kill 1,500 (we'll use the higher number that some C.O.s believe in). This means a total black bear kill of about 6,500. That is a total kill of less than 6% even if you use Ministry of Environment's conservative estimates. There would have to be well over 12,000 black bears killed each year just to hold the population in check .

The average kill for grizzlies, including hunter kill, C.O. kill, and Parks kill, is 350. There is probably about another unreported 40, and 20 for parts; that's a total of about 410. Using the Wildlife Branch numbers, this would mean a harvest of about 3-5%. The problem is that I know for certain that in the mid coast area of B.C., and in some other areas of the povince, the Wildlife Branch grizzly population estimates are far too low. The Wildlife Branch also uses a very low recruitment rate estimate, and a very high unreported kill rate estimate, for grizzly bears.

We could safely harvest over 500 grizzlies a year in B.C. if we used a point penalty system for reducing sow kills and targeted dominant cub-killing males and immigrant males.

The population of both bear species in B.C. will actually be increasing over the next 15 years because of the present level of protection and increased forage created by logging. After that, there will be a long, slow decline in populations because of an increase in mature-phase plantations, urbanization, and agriculture. But we are lucky; vast areas of B.C. are too rugged for agriculture and human growth potential - bears will survive well into the future. BEARS ARE NOT ENDANGERED IN B.C.

However, if 50 years from now there are 30 million people in B.C., there will be very few grizzly bears left. But this long-term pessimistic view does not justify the radical over-protection of bears at this time - it won't help them a bit. If a major grizzly population decline does eventually happen, it will *not* be caused by hunting, logging, mining, or petroleum exploration. It will be caused by a slow, continuous control kill of grizzlies in urban and agricultural growth areas because of human population growth.

HUMAN/BEAR CONFLICT

We are presently preserving and protecting bears in such a way that there are going to be more of them, and more of them that do not fear man. There is also a major effort by politicians in Canada to disarm the average citizen. This all points to more human/bear conflict.

Over the years I have worked on many projects to help protect bears and bear habitat, but my efforts have always been tempered with concepts for also protecting people from dangerous bears. Some biologists believe that we can manage grizzly bears for maximum-phase populations in all areas (like the Bella Coola Valley where there are 2,500 people) and not have increased danger to people. Of course, these biologists live in the city; they're not the people with bears in their backyard. I've got news for them: You can no more live with a grizzly in your backyard than you can live with cancer in your body - both entities are too dangerous to co-habit with.

British Columbians are killing fewer bears now than 20 years ago. Predatory type bears do not fear humans and often approach for a closer look. This type of bear used to be killed quickly, but no more. Thus you can expect more predatory attacks in the future.

Many people in our North American culture have strange concepts about bears and nature. Quite often I hear that people get attacked by bears because they are invading the bear's territory - as if it was the person's own fault. People should not approach nature as a dominant force ready to steamroll everything in their way. But people have as much right to live, work, and play in wild country as bears do - except in a bear preserve. We must come up with realistic ideas for protecting both people and bears.

If we are going to make an area a bear preserve only, then we must keep the people out - completely. If we're talking about a park for people and bears both, then some bear mortality will be necessary, as will strict fines for people who don't follow the rules.

I advocate that we protect bears at the species level, and protect people at the individual level. What this means is that we make sure that hunting harvest levels, problem bear kills, and habitat alteration do not substantially reduce bear populations within a management unit area. But we protect individual people by quickly killing dangerous bears and by using hunting as a way to reduce bear populations where necessary and to maintain bears' fear of people. In most areas there is too much emphasis on protecting individual bears, no matter how dangerous they are.

After talking to several thousand rural British

Columbians, and hearing their bear stories and opinions about human/bear conflict, I have come to believe that bears should be managed in B.C. to accomplish the following three primary goals:

1. To insure public safety by deliberately reducing bear populations by about 25% in parks and places where people and bears must co-exist.
2. To insure long-term bear species survival in as many areas as is feasible.
3. To provide economic benefits to British Columbians through resident and guided hunting.

Presently in B.C. there is precious little interest in managing bear populations for reducing bear danger to people and there seems to be a determined effort by the present government to eliminate hunting, especially trophy hunting.

A new law just came into effect this year (1994) that requires a hunter who has killed a black bear to remove and transport all of the edible portions of the carcass to his residence. Black bears are mainly hunted as a trophy species and this new law is utterly ridiculous. It will cause a significant reduction in the black bear hunter kill right at a time when the Ministry of Environment should be doing everything possible to increase the hunter kill because of the over-abundance of black bears in the province.

There are many more bears killed each year by other bears than by people. Trophy hunting kills are very humane compared to bear deaths that result from social regulatory pressure.

I hope that a majority of British Columbians become aware of the absurdity that is going on and demand that the government return to more realistic and sensible bear management policies.

12

Conservationism Versus Preservationism

In the previous chapter I demonstrated how bear management influences the frequency of bear attacks and human/bear conflict. There is another important factor that will influence how many people are killed and injured by bears in the future: *the politics of nature.*

Wildlife managers have to operate within the political priorities of the government in power. British Columbia has the most politicized Wildlife Branch of all the state and provincial authorities in North America, and the present government is determined to leave its mark on the Ministry of Environment.

For close to 50 years our cultural concepts dealing with nature have been based on the principles of conservation. We are now abandoning those principles and replacing them with radical concepts of preservation.

If the preservationists get their way, there will be so many bears in some areas, you won't be able to avoid them; if some politicians and bureaucrats also get their way, you won't be carrying a firearm to defend yourself with.

Consider this statement:

> B.C. bear status report: Even though there are
> some areas in the province where additional
> protection is needed for grizzly bears, both bear
> species are doing quite well. Grizzly
> populations have increased significantly in
> recent years in the mid coast area, the West
> Chilcotin, and in South Tweedsmuir Park. In
> many other areas of the province bear popula-
> tions are stable or increasing. Present evi-
> dence indicates that the new bear parts trade
> ban is helping to reduce the number of black
> bears being killed each year for bear parts.
> The Ministry of Environment, the B.C. Wild-
> life Federation, the provincial Rod & Gun
> Clubs, and the Conservation Officer Service
> should all be credited for the many conserva-
> tion projects, increased habitat protection, and
> the effective changes and enforcement of hunt-
> ing regulations that have brought about this
> improved picture for bears.
> *By James (Gary) Shelton*

The above statement is a very accurate assessment
of the bear situation in B.C. according to the
hundreds of field workers I talk to each year. But I
bet you haven't seen any articles like it in print.
Now read the following statement:

> Recent studies indicate that bears are in dan-
> ger of extinction in B.C. Sport hunters are
> destroying grizzlies by the hundreds for the
> sheer fun of it and, according to some Conser-
> vation Officers, the endless carnage of thou-
> sands of bears continues so that their gall blad-
> ders can be removed for illegal sale. Accord-
> ing to a study of grizzlies killed by residents on

the B.C. coast, there have been 367 grizzlies killed for dubious reasons in the last ten years. Can bears last to the turn of the century if this wholesale slaughter continues?
By a B.C. environment group

I have read between 40 and 50 items of this type in the last four years in various newspapers and magazines. The authors of these articles twist or fabricate information to meet their needs. Why do they do this? Because they believe their cause justifies any methods necessary to achieve their goals.

British Columbia is one of the main battle-grounds in the "international environmental wars" presently being fought. Considering the propaganda that is being put out by domestic and international environment groups, they must believe that "all is fair in love or war".

The concept that they are trying to ram down our throats is called "international environmental affirmative action." They claim that B.C. belongs to all of mankind and that British Columbians are mere custodians. We must set aside vast protected areas so that people from other areas of the world (who became wealthy by exploiting nature to extinction in their own countries) can come and experience real nature - here. They want us to stop hunting bears, to stop trapping, and to stop a good part of our mining and logging.

These preservationists are mounting an unrelenting attack right now because they know that our present government is wobbling at the knees and will most likely put politically-correct minority groups ahead of the majority of British Columbians.

Conservationism and preservationism are two totally different concepts. They are based on two very different philosophical foundations about the basic tenants of nature.

Most modern conservationists believe in a type of

natural world where a limited amount of balancing takes place, where competing destructive forces are at work, that mankind is an integral part of the system, and that our behaviour reflects nature. But we must reduce and limit our impact on wild systems whenever possible. This belief system is a stoic relic of the synthesis of Neo-Darwinism and Judeo-Christianity that took place in the late 1940s.

Most people who advocate preservationist doctrines believe in a "natural regime" where forces exist that balance, protect, and enhance individual species. An inter-connecting web of life exists where the loss of any species may cause an ecosystem disaster. The human behaviour of capitalistic-materialism was created by culture in the last 10,000 years and is a perversion of natural processes. This viewpoint is a modern version of the pro-nature anti-capitalist belief system that was born in the United States during the 1960s.

There is no doubt that humans have raised havoc with the world's biosphere, and we must limit that damage wherever possible. However, we must compare our transgressions to nature's present and past destructive forces to obtain a realistic view of how we can best protect nature and bears.

The time has come to add strength and clarity to the first part of this book. We must carefully determine which of the two belief systems is closer to reality. In order to do this, we must explore the problem at two different structural levels: first, the reality of how natural systems work, and second, the underlying reality of how human socio-economic activities influence those systems.

NATURE REALITY IN BRITISH COLUMBIA

During the last 15 years, many scientific studies have been done on various aspects of natural phenomena that will help us in our pursuit of a balanced and accurate view of reality. Studies on plate tectonics indicate that in the last million years, B.C. has been ruptured, uplifted, and significantly altered by volcanism. Studies of past glaciations tell us that B.C. has been pounded into submission four different times in the last million years by the crushing advance of ice that was 2000 metres thick in some places. Almost all life in British Columbia was extinguished for the 75,000 years' duration of the last ice-age, the one that ended about 14,000 years ago.

The most interesting recent studies that shed light on the pre-history of our province are the core samplings of muskegs, bogs, and lake bottom sediments that have been done in western Canada. Palynologists (fossil pollen specialist) drive a coring tool into the sediment to be tested, then remove and extract the sediment core. Material at spaced intervals of the sample is radiocarbon-dated to determine age, then plant pollen grains are extracted from all levels and studied for identification in order to obtain a pollen spectrum.

This type of research has shown that the lodgepole pine migrated from Southern B.C. to the Central Yukon from 12,000 to 400 years ago. It reached Central B.C. about 8,000 years ago. Other plant species show similar - but different time interval - northerly migrations. This migration followed the retreating ice as we entered the existing inter-glacial period. An archaeologist friend of mine from Vancouver, Phil Hobler, states that Western Red Cedar did not return to the mid coast of B.C. until about 4,500 years ago.

Scientists combine the pollen spectrum evidence with fossil evidence in order to discern a plant and animal mosaic of a certain area at a particular time in the past. The pollen spectrum also gives insights into the short-term and long-term changes in weather patterns.

During the last glacial episode, most of Alaska and

Eastern Eurasia was ice-free and connected by a land bridge. At that time ocean levels were 100 metres lower. This area called Beringia was isolated east and west by ice sheets, and had plant and animal species considerably different from North American species south of the ice.

By about 12,000 years ago, the ice had retreated enough for a major invasion of Beringian species into Western Canada. This was not the first invasion of this type; it had happened before in previous inter-glacial intervals. There was also an invasion by humans from Siberia at this time. It is believed that one previous human invasion by the same route may have also happened.

The most interesting piece of information that comes out of all of this scientific scrutiny is this: British Columbia has been altered, disrupted, crushed, and invaded to a more significant degree than just about anywhere else on earth.

Let's now put the pieces of the puzzle together: For eons, B.C. has been uplifted, ruptured, and altered by the collision and sub-duction of tectonic plates. Many areas of B.C. were destroyed and covered in the past by volcanic ash and lava flows. Four different times in the last 1,000,000 years, almost all life was crushed to smithereens by glacial advance. During each inter-glacial period, forest systems slowly moved northward, then back southward, creating ever-changing temporary equilibriums that favored or disfavored individual species. Each inter-glacial period had different mosaics of plant and animal communities; many only existed for short periods and never returned.

As the existing inter-glacial period we are now in began between 12,000 and 9,000 years ago, a wave of extinction eliminated between 35-40 large and small mammal species that were indigenous to North America. This was not the largest extinction wave of the last million years, but it was a significant one.

Some scientists claim that some of the larger mammals were killed off by primitive human hunters; some suggest that changing weather and changing environments were the culprits; others believe that North American species did not have resistance to Eurasian diseases. Probably all these causes were involved as there were also considerable extinctions of bird species and other types of lifeforms.

Even though we are now in a warming trend reversal, we have been into the next glacial period (neoglaciation) for about 4,500 years. Some forest systems have already retreated hundreds of kilometres southward, and most mountain timberlines have retreated hundreds of metres downward.

Some biologists believe that the Cassiar Mountains of northern B.C. have been becoming snowier and colder in the last 500 years, resulting in a decline of Stone Sheep populations. A 9,500-year-old Bighorn Sheep skull found in the Rocky Mountains indicates that this species ranged much farther north than its present range before our neo-glaciation started. This species has already started its long-term southerly migration.

Three hundred years ago, elk suffered extinction in the Chilcotin area of B.C., probably caused by the southerly intrusion of the sub-boreal pine/spruce forest into the montaine spruce forest system. Moose first arrived in the West Chilcotin in 1921. There had never been moose there before. This species had existed in sub-arctic areas of North America for thousands of years and quickly expanded its range throughout B.C. after the turn of the century because of vast drought-induced burns. The range expansion of this new species finally culminated in the late 1960s when the first moose arrived in the Uinta Mountains of Utah.

The Itcha Mountain Caribou herd (north of Anahim, B.C.) almost suffered extinction in the late 1970s because of heavy winters and wolf predation.

This herd is probably a remnant herd, and there is considerable evidence that caribou are presently being disfavored by natural forces in the southern half of B.C.

Elk are presently expanding their range in central B.C.; blacktail deer are increasing in population in the mid coast area; mountain goat populations on the coast are at all-time highs. These three trends are the result of 12 mild winters in a row, and will abruptly end with the next round of hard winters.

To put it mildly, this province has been in a long state of geophysical, climatic, and biological flux. If you live long enough, and are observant enough, you will see change in your lifetime.

Does this sound like a nature that balances, enhances, and protects individual species? Hardly. A belief system that advocates these principles is nothing more than a kind of pantheistic mythology. Unfortunately, practitioners of this cult have many sympathetic politicians and bureaucrats in the present B.C. government.

Let's now take a look at mankind's damage to nature in B.C.

We have considerably altered B.C. through urbanization, agriculture, mining, and hydro-electric development. But in the last 15 years, logging activities and petroleum exploration have altered the land more than anything else.

In the mid 1950s, the B.C. Forest Service started vigorous fire suppression in order to reduce the millions of dollars of losses due to wild fires. During the 1960s and 1970s, our rate of timber harvest was low enough that logging basically replaced fire as the rejuvenator of forests. Intensive tree planting had not yet been initiated, and logging slashes went through a long regeneration period that created tremendous forage for animals.

In the 1980s, the Timber Supply Area Steering

Committees were dominated by large logging and milling companies who recognized that the government had opened the door for a timber rush with the new Forest Act of 1978. Total watershed clear-cutting was allowed and our protective environmental guidelines were relaxed. In a mere ten years, logging radically altered vast areas of the southern two-thirds of the province. In the last 15 years we have created access to large areas of the northern one-third of B.C. by seismic-line road building activity in relation to gas and oil exploration.

The 1980s brought tremendous wealth to British Columbians, but the penalty will be loss of vast wild areas. The frontier days are over. We have now removed enough timber that we will have to bring on second-growth as fast as possible, or we will have a serious timber shortage in the not-too-distant future. This means silvicultural techniques that will shorten the herbaceous regeneration cycle, and a quick rotation of plantations before they become semi-open-canopy old-growth with forage. We have altered a large part of B.C. that will take several hundred years to recover.

WHAT DOES ALL THIS MEAN?

There never has been a "balanced natural regime" in B.C. as many people believe, and even if there had been, fire suppression, logging, and present restocking standards have changed vast areas of wildlife habitat. We must actively manage and husband all of our animal species if we are going to maintain strong, viable wildlife populations in British Columbia.

If wolf control, for example, was a wildlife management decision instead of a political decision, we could bring our caribou populations back quickly. If we managed wolf populations for a lower density, our hunting and guiding industries would prosper and return many more millions of dollars to the B.C. economy than they already do. If there was enough vision to leave about 5% of our interior logging slashes (with the right elevation and rainfall) for natural regeneration, our moose and deer populations would benefit much more from logging.

We are headed for an all-or-none concept of preservation: we save this area, and destroy that area. If our Ministry of Environment regional offices had the freedom and determination to actually use all the conservation techniques at their disposal, instead of sitting by in preservationist gridlock, we could radically increase the population of most of our animal species without seriously reducing logging, mining, or oil exploration. But as long as our government is controlled by people who believe in the fantasy that there is a "wonderful balanced regime" out there, our wildlife populations and related economic potential will continue to decline.

EXTENDED FIRST-PHASE ECONOMICS

The second level of analysis that we must undertake in order to determine whether the conservation philosophy or the preservation philosophy is more valid pertains to the socio-economic influences that affect nature. I call this system of analysis *extended first-phase economics*. This system explores the real underlying relationship of how economic activity affects nature, and who is really responsible for that effect.

Very few people ever carefully examine how economic systems really work. For example, if we set aside thousands of hectares of timber that can't be logged, and shut down our guiding industry for the unnecessary over-protection of grizzly bears, what is the total influence on the world besides the loss of millions of dollars to the B.C. economy?

The world demand for that timber will still be there.

Does this mean that the demand will be filled by logging valuable jaguar habitat in South America? Or will the timber be removed in an area where one of the Asian bears is endangered? It certainly won't come from spotted owl country.

Every product purchased in the world marketplace has elements in it that represent the destruction of habitat or the elimination of competitive plant and animal species somewhere in the world.

That's right, even all those things preservationists buy: their cars, their homes, their food, their clothes, their compact discs, and even their bean sprouts. Do preservationists refuse a hookup to B.C. Hydro in order to make sure they are not contributing to the electricity demand that devastated all those hectares of prime habitat flooded by dams? Do they refuse to live in dwellings that are constructed of lumber? Do they refuse to purchase fuel that originates from oil that is pumped from the ground in grizzly habitat?

It's wonderful to have bananas, tomatoes, and oranges any time of the year - and all those other cheap goods from areas of the earth where there are very few restrictions on agricultural or industrial expansion. But there is a cost for all this: Somewhere in the world, life is eliminated for our comfort. In other words, because you exist, you are causing death and destruction somewhere in the world right now.

Even though I'm a hunter and kill animals, there are many so-called environmentalists who consume far more world goods than I do, and as a result, they contribute to more total world destruction than I do.

We of course all want to reduce our negative impact on the natural world, but the unfortunate reality is this: *The only thing that will actually stop the continued destruction of world ecosystems is stopping human population growth.*

How much money have you seen radical

environmentalists spend lately towards that goal? Are they lobbying the Canadian federal government to reduce or stop immigration into Canada? Are they working to reduce the continued urban and agricultural growth? Are they spending time and money to promote birth control? Why do they keep spending millions of contributed dollars to fix the symptoms instead of treating the cause? Because they are socialists first, and environmentalists second.

If you carefully examine the issues that preservationists get involved in, you will find preservationists are doing little to help stop human population growth. They are targeting capitalism. They claim that corporate greed is causing all our problems. If we all went back to living in small cabins, living off the land, and sharing our wealth, everything would be okay.

Radical environmentalists have the classic Marxist view of history, economics, and human behaviour. They don't seem to know that large corporations can exist only if millions of people buy their products voluntarily.

The only way to stop the continuous environmental damage being done to the earth is to stop human population growth. But there is a big problem here. Economic growth in most industrialized nations is directly linked to human population growth. How do we disconnect the two? Should we let our economy collapse and go back to wearing animal fur, eating fish, and a life span of 28 years? If we did that, we would have to revert to a harsher system of capitalism than we now practise, and it would be devastating to the environment.

First-phase-economics is based on rudimentary principles of survival and safety. Before the second world war, Bella Coola Valley residents, to a degree, lived under this condition. They cut their own firewood, grew their own food, made most of their clothes (including wool garments), cut their own lumber, and created many other necessary products for survival. They also bought many products from "outside" like salt, cloth, tools, and machinery.

During this previous time, people here could not possibly live with maximum-phase populations of grizzlies, black bears, wolves, cougars, fox, mink, and hawks. You simply could not compete against these wild creatures; they would kill your livestock, eat your garden vegetables, and steal your eggs - they would destroy you economically and present danger to you and your family.

Bella Coola residents are now removed from a land-based existence enough that we can tolerate much higher populations of competing wildlife than our forebearers could. But this is only possible because we can now obtain cheap goods from other areas of the world, and we don't have to extract them directly from our own environment. But what effect does this have on those other areas of the world? Are we trading Asiatic black bears for grizzlies? Jaguars for spotted owls?

Why is it feasible for a B. C. logger to buy most of his vegetables from California rather than grow them himself? Because he can make good money in resource extraction, then buy cheap vegetables from farms in California where not only has the land been cleared, drained, and all competitive plant and animal species eliminated, but it has also been irrigated with water from vast diverted river systems. His decision is an economic one, and his decision directly reduces the demand to clear more land in B.C. - but increases the need to clear more land in California.

If all British Columbians went back to first-phase-economic living conditions right now, we would devastate all of the prime B.C. habitat in very short order. Our resource-removal-based economy is much less destructive to the environment in the long run than the industrial manufacturing and agricultural-based economies in the nations from which we import most of our goods.

Take a real close look at all those nations around the world where the majority of the population is still locked into first-phase economic living conditions. Look at how much habitat they must destroy just to feed themselves because they can't afford to develop or purchase our technology. These are the areas where most of the plant and animal extinctions are presently taking place.

British Columbians are lucky; we can trade very valuable resources to other nations for products that cause far more long-term damage to nature than our own resource extraction. We will be able to protect a reasonable portion of B.C., but only because we are willing to sacrifice other areas of the world's surface, along with the plant and animal species that live there. If we choose, we can allow many logged areas to eventually return to their previous condition, but we do not have the option of allowing urban and agricultural land to revert back to nature.

Preservationists not only believe in a mythology about nature, they also believe in a mythology about economics. They don't know that they are just as responsible for world destruction as you and I. They also have a mythology about human behaviour with their anti-capitalistic belief system. The very essence of human existence is to control and organize resources around us for survival. As modern, responsible capitalists we must use conservation to limit the destructive side of that powerful force, always remembering, however, that the constructive side of that force lifted us to being a creature who cares about other lifeforms.

No human culture can even consider the protection of wild species until it has created enough wealth, through economic enterprise, to lift itself above the limiting shackles of bare survival.

The fundamental principle of wildlife conservation is that all animals reproduce more individuals each year than can possibly survive. These surplus animals are a natural resource that we should harvest for our own benefit and for the purpose of reducing the amount of terrible deaths that result from over-population.

Our future in B.C. is in resource removal, and we should be happy about it. We just have to do it right; we must protect the environment by not over-harvesting any plant or animal species. We must use good sound conservation techniques. I sit on a land-use committee that is already a long way towards bringing this about in our area of influence. While most of the province was locked in bitter environmental debate, we slowly hammered out a realistic system of protecting our local economy and environment. We were able to accomplish our goals because we used the basic principle of democracy - that rare commodity in British Columbia nowadays: majority rule. Unfortunately, radical preservationists seem totally incapable of contributing to this process because they are unwilling to compromise - the kind of compromise that every person who sits on the Bella Coola Local Resource Use Plan Committee is willing to make.

The Hong Kong money that has been coming into and bolstering the B.C. economy will eventually dry up, and it will be 20 to 30 years before tourism plays a major role in our economy. We must not destroy our present economic base, as preservationists would have us do.

13

Conclusion

In the first part of this book we carefully explored bear aggressive behaviour and the best strategies for avoiding injury or death during a bear encounter. The second part was an examination of bear management concepts and our cultural beliefs about nature.

I could not have presented the Bear Encounter Survival Guidelines in this book during the present environmental warfare without first laying out a long and tedious foundation of what they are based on. But much of the material in that long and tedious foundation tore up new ground, and some of it sacred ground.

High priests of that holy ground - the preservationists - will scramble to protect the dogma. I could not have left any scripture of misinformation unchallenged, or they would try to use it to exorcise the demon (me). No matter how many human lives this book saves, I will have committed heresy to those who place animals and nature above humanity.

The present "international environmental wars" being fought in British Columbia have taken a serious toll on our economy. Many environmental groups are working hard to convince European countries and the U.S. to boycott B.C. lumber products. Our Premier has traveled to Europe to try to limit the potential economic damage that a boycott could cause. He has tried to explain that we have changed our ways and are now doing a much better job of protecting the environment. But he will have to keep his travel bags packed.

Our province has another problem: During the last four years of local environmental conflict we have dismantled our land-use decision-making mechanism and are in the process of recreating it. This is a vulnerable time when fanatics on both sides of issues distort and misrepresent information in order to sway the general public. Unfortunately, many people around the world do not understand that B.C. is very different from Germany or Brazil. We have unique problems here that must be sorted out by British Columbians.

B.C. has some of the most magnificent, unspoiled landscape on earth. When the battle is finally over, there will no doubt be more areas set aside for future generations. But it would appear that B.C. has been targeted as the area of the planet where we will make up for all of man's past transgressions against nature.

There is a real danger that absurd, extreme over-protection of bears may end up as an appeasement bargaining chip when the final peace accord is negotiated in the near future.

If this happens, our economy will lose millions of dollars each year - unnecessarily - because of reduced hunting, guiding, mining, and logging activity. This absurd over-protection of bears will also cause an increase in human/bear conflict and bear attacks on British Columbians.

We must muster the determination to create our own future by limiting external influences, making sure that the information we use for important land-use and wildlife management decisions is factual and unbiased.

There are three important elements for reducing

human/bear conflict: good practical information, sound bear management strategies, and realistic political decisions. It's not enough to teach people about surviving bear encounters; we must also manage bears in a sensible way.

Many biologists and politicians have been operating as if there is no connection between the way we manage bears and the frequency of bear attacks on people. There is a direct relationship between the two, and the time has come for North Americans to reconsider the unnecessary and dangerous drift towards preservationism.

We must manage bears for human safety first, and bear safety second. This is not possible unless we reverse present trends.

During the last five years many people have asked me how high is the risk of being attacked by a bear. I tell people to disregard statistical statements about bear attacks, such as the comparison of bear attacks to lightning strike deaths. If over 50% of North Americans are exposed to lightning strike danger, and less than 1% of the population exposed to bear attack danger, then the two are not statistically comparable.

For some people, such as Fisheries personnel who do creek walks in highly populated grizzly areas, or field workers in the northeast part of the province who often encounter predacious black bears, the risk of attack is fairly high. But for the average British Columbian, driving a car, riding an ATV, or riding a horse is much more dangerous than hiking through bear country. But I have learned something important during the last six years of delivering my bear safety courses: People have long ago accepted the risk of driving a car, riding an ATV, or riding a horse, but nobody ever gets used to the idea of having a bear take them down and remove half their face, no matter what level of risk is involved.

The fear of being attacked by a bear hits a psychic chord that brings panic to most people well beyond the dread of other types of danger. I have rarely felt fear during a bear encounter, but I have felt terror shortly after some of the sow grizzly encounters that I've had. Grizzly bears are specialists at terrorizing an intruder, and anyone who has experienced that feeling knows why the fear of bear attacks is not related to the comparatively low level of risk.

The bear stories that I have included in this book represent a small portion of what is actually taking place in B.C., and a drop in the bucket of what is going on in North America. If anyone out there has a bear story, old or new, please put it down accurately on paper or tape, and mail it to me. I can use this very important information for helping to reduce bear danger to people. Include a statement to the effect that I can use your story in my bear hazard safety training program, or in future publications.

Respectfully,

James (Gary) Shelton
Box 95
Hagensborg, B.C.
Canada V0T 1H0

P.S. I did not include many human death stories in this book because I did not want the tragedy element of these incidents to influence the technical nature of this material. But this book only paints part of the picture of human/bear conflict; my next book, to be published in 1997, will complete that picture by showing the horrific nature of bear attacks.